END OF
VOYAGES

THE AFTERLIFE OF A SHIP

END OF
VOYAGES

THE AFTERLIFE OF A SHIP

MICHAEL STAMMERS

TEMPUS

First published 2004

Tempus Publishing Ltd
The Mill, Brimscombe Port
Stroud, Gloucestershire GL5 2QG
www.tempus-publishing.com

British Library Cataloguing in Publication Data.
A catalogue record for this book is available from the British Library.

ISBN 0 7524 2999 X

Typesetting and origination by Tempus Publishing.
Printed and bound in Great Britain.

CONTENTS

ACKNOWLEDGEMENTS

I must acknowledge the kindness of all the people and organisations that have let me both have and use many of the photographs in this book. Some I have not been able to trace and apologies go to anyone who has been omitted. The more recent photographs are my own. The following should be mentioned: the late Jack Abel; Bristol Industrial Museum; Richard Compton-Hall of the RN Submarine Museum; Arthur Credland of Hull Maritime Museum; Valerie Fenwick; Jim Forrester; the late Alex Hurst; Lancaster Maritime Museum; Tony Lewery; Michael McCaughan of the Ulster Folk & Transport Museum; Campbell McCutcheon; the late Admiral Sir Patrick Bayly of the Maritime Trust; Hilton Matthews; Chris Millward; Mark Myers; National Museums Liverpool; the late Edward Paget-Tomlinson; the late Jack Parkinson; John Smith of the Falklands Trust and Museum; the late Peter Throckmorton; the Viking Ship Museum, Roskilde; Nick Walker of VIC 32; Colin Wilkinson.

Finally, I make no apologies for the choice of ships. So far as possible I have picked ships and boats that I have seen. These reflect the fact that I have spent much of my time on the Mersey and travelled to places like the Falkland Islands. I have also tried to pick some ships that are perhaps not the most famous or obvious examples. If anyone wants to follow up the story of any of the ships in the text there are references to more detailed works in the bibliography.

CHAPTER ONE

SHIPS DOWN THE AGES:
THEIR 'BIRTHS' AND 'LIVES'

Ships are the biggest of all man-made moving objects. They have always been subject to all kinds of stresses and strains as they make their way through an ever moving, ever changing and often hostile environment – the sea. Landfall brings more hazards, such as unseen rocks and shallows. Then there are human hazards – war, piracy or plain human error – all of which can lead to complete destruction. Assuming it survives such dangers, a ship is also worn out through use. A wooden hull consists of many small components fastened together with wooden pegs, iron nails or bolts. Over time these loosen and wear. Marine boring creatures such as the teredo bore into the fabric, and fungal rot consumes a ship's strength from inside. Unless the owner is conscientious and carries out repairs regularly, the whole structure will fall apart and have to be discarded. The same is true for metal-hulled craft; rust (the oxidation of iron or steel) has to be kept in check by painting and by fitting sacrificial anodes to stop electrolytic action. Welds or rivets can fail and hulls can split apart.

Even if a ship is well looked after and not irreparably damaged or sunk by weather, rocks or attack, the usual end is destruction. Ships are normally broken up and their materials recycled. In some cases, where the effort of breaking up is too great or there is no market for scrap, the ship is simply abandoned and left to rot. This is particularly true for ships with wooden hulls, where the numerous iron fastenings make them difficult to take apart. In a few cases, the ship can be put to a different use from its original purpose. This is often in a stationary role such as a houseboat or a storage hulk. But there are a few survivors, ships that are deemed to be so important in national history – such as HMS *Victory* – that they are preserved. There are also many fragments of ships that have been saved. Figureheads are among the most important, for they are seen to embody the soul of the ship.

It may sound strange to write of an inanimate object as having a soul but, since the earliest days of seafaring, ships have been treated as animate beings. Each one, though they may be of a standard design, performs slightly differently when at sea. Most carry an individual name, not a number like an aircraft or a railway locomotive.

The Liverpool barque *Jhelum* lies derelict and abandoned in the Falkland Islands. After a sailing career lasting from 1849 to 1869, it became a storage hulk and workshop until the 1960s.

Such names can be based on abstract spiritual values such as Hope, Charity or Grace; they can be named after particular individuals such as James Baines, Mary Cairns or Pudge (a favourite daughter's pet name); they can be named in a series, such as Cunard's liners which took their names from provinces of the Roman Empire; or they can be as poetic as Skimmer of the Seas or as prosaic as Grit. Whatever the name may be, there is invariably a naming ceremony when the ship is launched. Indeed the metaphor has been extended; for example, the River Clyde has been described as 'the birth place of great ships'. Ships are also female. Although the Editor of the shipping paper *Lloyd's List* decreed in 2002 that his reporters would henceforth describe ships as 'it', most writers still use 'she'. Ships also sail on 'maiden voyages', have 'sister ships', 'careers' and 'adventures'. Particular types of ship are often written up in the most romantic terms. We hear of 'tall ships', 'clippers' and 'great liners' and yet all of these types were basically only an unromantic means to an end: to transport goods and people across the oceans and seas of the world. Nevertheless, the interest in ships, especially ships of the past, remains and continues to grow. There are whole museums solely devoted to ships and maritime affairs, and there are complete ships lovingly preserved. There is a keen market in ship relics, from pieces of equipment and fittings, to paintings, photographs and models. The great auction houses hold

Ships work in a hostile environment and need constant maintenance, otherwise they soon deteriorate – a fact that many ship preservationists like to ignore. Here rust is being chipped from the wrought-iron plating of the three-masted barque *Elissa*, built in Aberdeen in 1877. It is still afloat and sailing out of Galveston, Texas.

Old ships and boats had and continue to have an enormous following. Some people follow the practical route of restoring and sailing old boats or building models; others are content to read about them or take a cruise or day excursion. Specialist magazines such as *Ships and Ship Models: A Magazine for all Lovers of Ships and the Sea* was founded in 1931 to cater for the ship enthusiast.

regular maritime sales. Then there are new books about ships, both non-fiction and fiction, and even publishing firms specialising in shipping books. There are societies and magazines dedicated to the study of ships, especially ships of the past. They range from the general, such as the World Ship Society's newsletters, to the very specific, such as the *Titanic* Historical Society. The latter manage to publish a substantial journal every quarter. Then there are publications packed with 'How to' articles, such as *Classic Boat* and *Boatman*, dedicated to those who are mad enough to want to restore and maintain old wooden sailing boats. There are also journals for those who want to build models and magazines which combine news with articles about ships of the past. The oldest British survivor is *Sea Breezes*, which started as the house journal of the Pacific Steam Navigation Co. in 1919. Throughout the 1920s and the 1930s its circulation grew and the title was bought by a commercial publishing company. At that time it actually had the sub-title 'The Ship-Lover's Magazine'. Introducing the word 'lover' might have been taking things too far, but it was an indication of the depth of emotion ships could provoke. Clearly anyone who had served on a particular ship and had enjoyed happy times while on board would remember that vessel with affection and might go so far as to buy a book, photograph, painting, model or some other souvenir. But then there are others who are either simply interested in or enthusiastic about ships, and this can take many forms, from collecting 'the last remains' to helping to preserve a particular vessel either as a member of a society or as a personal crusade. For example, there are societies that have not only saved a vessel but continue to operate it. Among the most successful is the Paddle Steamer Preservation Society, which operates two paddle steamers, the *Waverley* and the *Kingswear Castle*, plus the vintage motor ship *Balmoral* on coastal and river excursions every summer.

Most of the vessels or bits of vessels covered in the succeeding chapters date from the last three centuries. However the last remains of a vessel can provide evidence about the development of ships in the centuries before there were any plans, documents and survivors. Most are shipwrecks or ships that have been abandoned and then covered with a preserving layer of mud. A few, like the Sutton Hoo ship, were deliberate burials for a religious purpose. What is more, the objects found on board such shipwrecks can act as a time capsule vividly illuminating how the crew lived and worked in a specific era. They can also be important for understanding the life and culture of a specific era on land where similar objects have not survived. Nautical archaeology, the study of the last remains of ships, has opened whole new insights into our past.

As a framework for the later chapters, it is worth including a brief overview of how ships developed. The first mariners probably used hollowed-out tree trunks as boats, which were satisfactory on inland waters and indeed are still in use in some parts of the world today. All over Europe log boats have been found sealed away from the degrading properties of oxygen in muddy deposits in rivers and lakes. Radioactive carbon dating and tree ring analysis have enabled us to date these last remains accurately and they can range from the Stone Age to the Middle Ages. The next stage was the addition of side planks to make the boat more seaworthy.

One of Man's oldest ways of getting afloat is the hollowed-out tree trunk. Many dug-outs have been excavated around the British Isles that date back to prehistoric times. Dug-outs are still built and are often beautifully shaped, like this West African example.

From there it is quite a long step to a large, fully structured hull powered by sails, but we can see this in Britain in the surviving remains of ships of the Roman occupation from the first to the fifth centuries AD. The Angles, the Saxons and the other Scandinavians who settled in Britain brought with them a different boatbuilding technique to produce long, seaworthy ships that could be rowed or sailed and which could operate in both shallow estuaries and deep seas. This form used overlapping planks fastened together, with the stiffening frames inserted after the hull had been fabricated. There were many detailed differences in the way clinker-built ships were constructed, but they remained the predominant type of ship in Britain until the fifteenth century.

It is difficult to be precise about the dates of changes in design and building but the carrack, with a full internal skeleton of framing timbers and a smooth outer skin of carvel planking and two or more masts, was certainly in evidence by 1400. It was influenced by Mediterranean shipbuilding techniques and provided European explorers with a vehicle in which to cross the Atlantic and circumnavigate the world. They also embodied a new departure in naval warfare. In the Middle Ages, there were very few specialised warships except for rowing galleys. Merchant ships were fortified with 'castles' at the bow and stern and packed with soldiers to attack the enemy. We still use the term 'forecastle' (or the shortened foc'sle) for the raised section at the bow of a ship.

Jumping forward many centuries, the Roman merchant ship had a large hull built from planks fastened edge to edge (carvel-built) on a set of frames. It was also capable of being sailed rather than powered by paddles or oars and could carry large amounts of cargo over long distances.

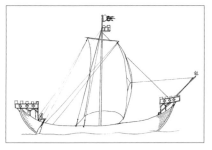

Whether carvel-built in the Mediterranean style or clinker-built in the various Northern European traditions, medieval ships developed in size and sophistication. This thirteenth-century English ship (engraved with the seal of the port of Winchelsea) had a deck, a winch for hauling up the sail and anchor, and the beginnings of permanent structures at the bow and the stern which were forts to defend the ship and fire on the enemy.

The ships of the Scandinavians, who raided and settled in Britain after the departure of the Romans, built ships with overlapping planking (clinker-built) with strengthening frames inserted inside the hull. These two replicas of cargo-carrying 'knarrs' are based on the remains of eleventh-century ships found near Roskilde, Denmark.

The invention of gunpowder and the development of cannon and their use at sea changed naval tactics. Ships could fight each other at long range and could be sunk by damaging the hull. Specialised armed battleships and full-time navies began to be established, although in peace time many of these expensive vessels would be laid up for care and maintenance. Merchant vessels, particularly those venturing in seas infested with pirates such as the Mediterranean or the Caribbean, also had guns as a means of self-defence.

The carrack was superseded by the galleon towards the end of the sixteenth century. This was a more seaworthy vessel, and this in turn developed into the classic three-masted, square-rigged ship, which had several square sails on each mast and fore and aft sails on the bowsprit (the spar that projects forward from the bow) and between the masts. This combination of sails made the vessel more manoeuvrable when going to windward. The average size of a deep-sea vessel also increased from an average of about 100 to 150 tons at the end of the seventeenth century to double that by the early 1800s. Warships and specialised traders, such as the ships of the East India Co., were often much larger.

By 1600 the sailing battleship had emerged with a heavy broadside armament of muzzle-loading guns arrayed on two or three decks and this became the norm for

The fourteenth and fifteenth centuries saw the development of much larger ships built with a heavy internal 'skeleton' of frames, up to four masts rigged with a combination of square and fore and aft sails and large integrated superstructures at the bow and stern. These carracks were part of Henry VIII's navy; indeed his *Mary Rose*, which sank in the Solent in 1545 and was raised at Portsmouth in 1982, is a carrack.

Above: Carracks and their successors, the galleons, were capable of long-distance voyages and were essential to the European explorers. The *Golden Hind* is a modern replica of Sir Francis Drake's ship which sailed round the world between 1577 and 1580. It gives a good idea of the layout and rig of a galleon.

Left: The large carrack design also made it possible to carry an armament of muzzle-loading cannon, mounted on either side of the hull. The design developed into the massive wooden 'ships of the line' of the eighteenth and early nineteenth century. Nelson's flagship at the Battle of Trafalgar in 1895, HMS *Victory,* is a prime example and carried 100 guns on three decks.

European nations with full-rigged ships extended trade and established colonies in all parts of the world. The mid-Atlantic island of St Helena became a British possession in 1673 and had a strategic value on the long route to South Africa and India.

the next two and a half centuries. These 'wooden walls' were displaced by 'ironclads' – steam-powered, iron-hulled warships – from the 1850s onwards.

The merchant sailing ship reached its peak in the mid-nineteenth century. There were large, fast, wooden ships of the mid-nineteenth century intended for specific, highly profitable trades such as carrying emigrants and supplies to the Gold Rushes in California and Australia or bringing tea back from the Far East. Then there were also new iron ships that developed into carriers of bulk cargoes such as coal and grain. The last deep-sea sailing ships were massive steel, four-masted barques that could carry up to 5,000 tons of cargo. They could be sailed by a small crew with the assistance of various labour-saving pieces of equipment such as an auxiliary steam engine for hoisting anchors.

The nineteenth century also saw the development of a wide range of coastal and inshore craft around the British Isles. Many, such as the Norfolk wherry – a type of sailing barge – had their origins in the distant past but reached their peak of development in Queen Victoria's time. Although steamships were working reliably by the 1840s, sailing ships remained common until the First World War, though in declining numbers.

The earliest steamers were canal boats powered by paddles. The one that is generally recognised as the very first was a catamaran with one paddle fitted between the two hulls in 1788. The first practical steamer, the *Charlotte Dundas*, was tried out successfully on the Forth & Clyde Canal in 1802. However, it was stopped from realising its commercial potential by the canal owners, who feared it would wash away the canal's banks. 1812 saw the launch of the first seagoing steamer, the *Comet*, at Dumbarton. The next decade saw the rapid expansion of steamer services for passenger, mail and high-paying freight all around the British Isles and thereafter extending to services to continental ports. The technology had progressed so much that by the late 1830s it was possible to consider bridging the Atlantic Ocean by steamship.

This ushered in not only an increase in size but also the use of a new material, wrought iron, for the hull and a screw propeller instead of paddles. These new advances were embodied in Isambard Brunel's *Great Britain* of 1843.

Steamers still suffered from major drawbacks, however. They were expensive to build and their inefficient low-pressure boilers needed huge amounts of coal. Coal displaced cargo space and many early steamers could only pay their way by being supported by government subsidy in the form of payments for carrying mail. Possible solutions began to be practicable by the late 1850s and these included redesigning the boiler to accept a higher steam pressure, using the steam to work twice in a high- and then a low-pressure cylinder and by being able to recycle their steam by using a condenser. Alfred Holt, who was a trained engineer and a Liverpool ship-owner, demonstrated the practicality of high-pressure boilers and compound engines by building three steamers in 1865 capable of steaming 8,000 miles without refuelling, This enabled his firm to compete with the China clippers for valuable Far East trade.

In some ways warships changed radically: iron hulls and steam power were accepted and some warships had heavy calibre guns mounted in revolving turrets instead of the old 'broadside' arrangement. At the same time (for the Royal Navy at least) there was a reluctance to give up sails and rely entirely on steam power.

New kinds of ships were developed to carry new cargoes. Oil was originally carried in barrels or tins in sailing ships. By 1890 there were tankers that carried this increasingly important commodity in bulk. Other vessels were fitted with refrigerating equipment to carry such perishable foodstuffs such as meat from South America or Australia. Steel, a far stronger and lighter material, displaced wrought iron as the main material for shipbuilding.

In the early twentieth century steam turbines and diesel engines were successfully applied to ships. The pioneer steam-turbine vessel built by Charles Parsons in 1894, the *Turbinia*, has been preserved at Newcastle upon Tyne's Discovery Museum. Ships increased in size and the largest of them were the great transatlantic liners such as the Cunard Line's *Mauretania* and *Lusitania* of 1907. Warship designers had also taken on these new developments to build bigger, faster battleships, starting with HMS *Dreadnought* of 1906, with heavier armour and larger-calibre guns than ever before. Although these were considered the peak of naval power at the time, the future lay in other technologies that were being developed in the same era – submarines and aircraft.

Top: The clipper ships like the *Champion of the Seas* of 1854 are considered to be the high point in merchant sailing ships. They were designed for speed to compete for high-paying cargoes. *Champion of the Seas* was built in 1854 at Boston by Donald McKay, one the leading American shipbuilders of his era for the Liverpool-Australia Black Ball Line.

Above: The first steamers used paddles rather than a screw propeller. The low steam pressure of their boilers and the size of their engines made it difficult to make them pay as commercial vessels. Samuel Cunard's transatlantic liners were viable because they had a government subsidy to carry mail. Cunard's *Arabia* was built in 1853 and, at 2,402 tons, was one the biggest ships afloat. By the 1860s screw propellers had proved themselves superior to paddles for deep-sea voyages. In 1864 it was sold, the engines and boilers taken out, and it was re-rigged as a pure sailing ship – a common conversion for the early steam liners.

Paddles made a ship more manoeuvrable than a propeller and tugs. Ferries and coastal passenger steamers all continued to be built with paddles until the late nineteenth century. The *Taff* was built by Stotherts at Bristol in 1856 and operated on a passenger and cargo service between Portishead, Newport and Cardiff.

Oil was found to be a more efficient fuel and easier to handle than coal, and many steamers were converted to burn it, but diesel engines were not common until after the 1930s. Early types of diesel engine were often mechanically complicated and not especially reliable. A landmark in their progress towards universal acceptance was the building of two 27,000-ton liners, the *Britannic* and the *Georgic*, with twin diesels instead of turbines in 1930 and 1932. Diesel propulsion is the predominant form of propulsion for merchant ships today and their reliability and fuel economy has been greatly improved since the oil crisis of the 1970s. Steam turbines are still found in liquefied gas tankers and in warships such as nuclear submarines where atomic reactions are used to generate heat to raise the steam. Gas turbines (the marine version of jet engines) are commonly fitted in warships, often in conjunction with diesels, and diesel-electric propulsion is also a common propulsion for the new generation of cruising liners.

The Second World War put a huge strain on the British merchant fleet. Many ships were sunk in the Battle of the Atlantic and replacements could only be delivered by the adoption of simplified standard designs and welding hulls instead of the traditional fastening method of riveting. These mass-production methods became standard practice in the post-war era and their diligent application enabled new shipbuilding countries – first Japan and then Korea – to take over from Britain as the chief supplier of ships to the world. Larger, more specialised ships were developed to cater for the increasing volume of world trade. The demand for oil grew and very large tankers of up to half a million tons capacity were launched to help transport crude oil from the wells (mainly in the Middle East) to refineries in the USA and Europe. Traditional tramp steamers carrying perhaps 10,000 tons of grain, metal ores or coal were replaced by bulk carriers which ranged from small ones or 'handymax' of 20,000 to 45,000 tons to Cape-size monsters of 200,000 tons. Cargo liners that had carried more expensive freights such as textiles and other manufactures have been displaced by container ships which carry cargo in standard-sized boxes that are 'inter-modal', i.e. they can be carried by road, rail or sea. Wheeled vehicles are now carried on roll-on roll-off ships (ro-ros).

By the 1880s steamers had taken over all the high-paying freights from sailing ships. High-pressure boilers and engines which used the steam twice (compounds) or three times (triple expansion) in larger metal hulls made profitable voyages to distant ports possible. Coaling stations and the shortcut of the Suez Canal added to their advantages. Cargo liners plied on regular routes while tramp steamers worked voyage by voyage usually with bulk cargoes such as coal. The Blue Funnel liner *Diomed* of 1917 can be taken as typical, with engines and accommodation amidships (though with the crew berthed at the stern) and four cargo holds with plenty of cargo-handling derricks on either side.

At the start of the twentieth century competition between shipping companies of different nations was intense, especially in the transatlantic passenger trade. Record-breaking voyages attracted publicity and passengers. In 1907, the Cunard Line (with government support) stole a march with the introduction of the *Mauretania* and the *Lusitania*, which were bigger and faster than any other ships. Their speed was due to their innovative steam turbine engines, which rapidly became standard propulsion for fast liners and warships.

Warships changed out of all recognition between 1850 and 1900. In 1850 most of the world's navies consisted of wooden battleships similar to HMS *Victory*. By 1900, warships were built of steel with armour plating and fitted with breech-loading guns which could hurl explosive shells several miles. This Edgar class cruiser of 1893-94 was a successor of the old sailing frigate that could be used for protecting merchant shipping and scouting ahead of the main battle fleet.

In any era the building of a ship was a big expense and it normally called for people with specific expertise to construct the hull and make the equipment and fittings. There were also certain essential requirements in terms of location and access to water. In the case of a small wooden sailing ship these were relatively simple. There needed to be a firm sloping stretch of shore on which to set up the blocks on which the ship would be built; enough water in which to launch the completed hull; a quay or somewhere secure where the ship could be fitted with its masts and spars; ready access to supplies of timber, preferably oak; space around the building berth for storing timber and building a saw pit for cutting planks and frames; a blacksmith's shop and a hut for storing tools. All the work was carried out in the open and this was the same for the assembly of metal–hulled ships until fairly recently.

Designing the ship involved the use of a half model to delineate the shape from which the specific shape and measurements of the frames could be scaled up. The half model could represent the collective wisdom of generations of master shipwrights, thus embodying much experience on their part. Then there were rules about how the tonnage of a ship was measured for its official registration. For example, the depth of a ship was not taken into consideration in the measurements up to 1835, which made for ships with deep hulls, and there were also the rules of classification societies such as Lloyd's Register, which laid down the sizes of timbers

It was the new types of warship such as the aircraft carrier and the submarine that changed naval warfare in the twentieth century. Submarines equipped with torpedoes and using petrol or diesel engines on the surface and electric motors when submerged, were well developed by the outbreak of the First World War, and the German submarines such as the UC5 – a coastal minelayer – devastated British merchant shipping. Their many victims included the *Lusitania*, torpedoed off Ireland in May 1915.

for specific tonnages of ships. Iron and later steel ships needed more complicated facilities with expensive metalworking machinery, specialised forges, foundries, woodworking and electrical workshops, boiler-making and engine-erecting shops, rail access for bringing steel plates and bars and probably employing several thousand men. The designing of vessels became a more complex process. There was a new profession of naval architect who used mathematics to calculate strengths and shapes, and models were often built and tested in specially built test tanks to predict the characteristics of the proposed design. Detailed and accurate plans were drawn up in the drawing office and, as many copies were needed, they had to be duplicated. The most common copying process before the Xerox were drawings with white lines against a blue background – hence the word blueprint, which has passed into common use for any kind of master plan. Half models were still used for working out how the steel plates of hulls were to be positioned. Today, this kind of planning can be done in three dimensions on a computer using a CAD (computer-aided design) programme. The whole of the internals of the ship can be plotted out to make the best use of the space to ensure pipe work and cables etc. do not conflict with other equipment or fittings. The computer can also be used to programme cutting machinery that can cut steel plate in the most economical way and with great accuracy – a far cry from a man with an adze and pit saw.

New types of merchant ship also emerged at the end of the nineteenth century, such as the cargo ships with refrigerated holds to carry perishable cargoes such as meat and fruit. The most important design for the future was the bulk oil tanker, which could deliver crude oil from the oil wells to the refineries. The world's dependence on oil has grown massively and tankers have increased in size (up to 500,000 tons) and numbers. They were among the first ships to have their engines and accommodation at the stern (because of the fire risk). This layout is common to almost all cargo ships today.

The Second World War and the invasion of Europe produced innovations in handling wheeled cargo. Roll-on roll-off ferries which can carry cars and lorries via bow- and stern-loading doors have replaced the traditional cross-Channel ferry. The Finnish ro-ro *Leo* is unloading bulk paper via a floating ramp which connects up with its stern doors.

The completion of a ship and its launch is a special time and marked with a ceremony. In the case of a large liner or a warship, there would be an elaborate ceremony with bunting, a band and a platform party of VIPs, a brief service of blessing and perhaps a female member of the royal family to send the traditional bottle of champagne smashing into the bows to christen the ship with the recognised formula: 'I name this ship ... And God bless all who sail in her'. Even the launch of a humble Mersey sailing barge drew a crowd and was a cause for celebration. For example, the *Warrington Guardian* of 11 June 1879 reported that a large number of people gathered to watch the launch of the flat (barge) *Edith Mary* at Hill & Grundy's yard on the St Helen's Canal at Fiddler's Ferry. The flat was gaily dressed with flags and sixty or seventy people on board. At a signal given by the foreman shipwright, the wedges holding the barge on the slipways were knocked away and it slid gently sideways into the canal. Afterwards, there was a lunch of 'Old English fare' including rounds of beef and legs of mutton and 'the usual plum pudding' for the shipyard workers, barge skippers and owners, followed by toasts to the success of the vessel and to the Queen and Country.

Although we have stressed the hazards, some vessels survived through good building or rebuilding, or good fortune, for a very long time. HMS *Victory*, for example, was originally laid down at Chatham Naval Dockyard in 1759, launched in 1765, completed for service in 1778 and retained as an active warship until 1835. After this it became the stationary flagship which it remains today (although permanently in dry dock now). *Victory* also happened to be Lord Nelson's flagship at the Battle of Trafalgar in 1805 and his death during that battle made it a national and naval shrine. Less distinguished wooden warships have also survived for over a century, such as HMS *Unicorn*, a frigate also built at Chatham in 1824 and never commissioned. It has been a drill ship for reservists and is now actively preserved at Dundee. Some smaller vessels which have been used in hard commercial trades have also had remarkably long careers. The ketches *Good Intent* built at Plymouth in 1790, *William* built in 1809 at Bower Yard, Shropshire, and *Ceres* built at Salcombe in 1811 were all carrying heavy cargoes such as coal around the Bristol Channel well into the 1930s. Elsewhere the Mersey flat *Daresbury*, which had been built in 1772, was still afloat as a lifting barge on the Weaver Navigation until 1956. But for all these and other long-term survivors, there were hundreds of other vessels which at the end of their main working careers were converted to new uses such as static storage hulks. For those hundreds, there were thousands more which were wrecked, sunk, broken up or simply abandoned to rot. Nevertheless some of these survive as relics – pieces of equipment or ornament, for example – or have been reduced to miniature form in models, or memorialised in pictures or photographs. And, of course, there are even a few that have been saved as historic ships.

Left above: Since the 1960s, the use of standard-size containers which can be quickly loaded on ships, railway wagons or lorry trailers has revolutionised the deep-sea liner trades. One container ship displaced about six conventional cargo liners and could be loaded much more quickly than the 'break bulk' where all the miscellaneous items took much time to load and discharge. This German container ship is a small one for European routes. The biggest ones of the Sealand-Maersk Line can carry as many as 8,000 containers.

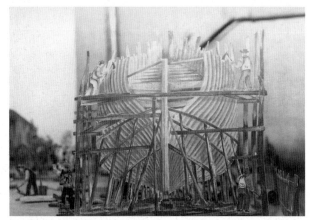

Left: Shipbuilding has changed: before 1850 most ships were built out of wood with a few metal fittings. This model of a Norfolk shipyard of 1847 shows a ship's frames and keel (its skeleton) erected awaiting the planking. All these components were skilfully fashioned by hand in the open on the building slip.

Above: The launch of a ship is a special occasion. It is both one for celebration and one for anxiety for the shipyard workers because for many this will be the end of their current work. Most ships go though a fitting-out stage and trials before their final handover. Launching ceremonies can be grand affairs attracting large crowds. Such was the case with the launch of the Cunard's second ship *Mauretania* at Cammell Laird's shipyard, Birkenhead, on 28 July 1938 by Lady Bates, the wife of the line's chairman.

Opposite below: By contrast, a modern shipyard will work with steel which is cut out by computer-guided machinery and welded together, all under cover. After completion, the hull is floated out rather than being launched in the traditional way. In this picture, two tugs are under construction in the IHC shipyard at Kinderdijk in 1993.

Some vessels can survive for a remarkably long time. The ketch *Good Intent* was launched at Plymouth in 1790 and was still carrying coal and other cargoes around the Bristol Channel well into the 1930s. It will have had several major refurbishings during its long and hard trading career.

The flat *Daresbury* was even older than the *Good Intent*. It was built at Northwich in 1772 and was still afloat in 1956. Built as a sailing cargo barge plying between the Weaver Navigation and Liverpool, it was rebuilt and lengthened in 1802. Eventually it lost its sails and was used as a maintenance and lifting barge. The *Daresbury* came out of service in 1956 and its rotting remains can still be seen sunk in the old Sutton Level lock on the Weaver.

Opposite above: Even humble vessels were celebrated, such as this wooden Mersey flat about to be launched at Abel's Castle Rock shipyard at Runcorn in 1915. The workforce and the owners can be readily distinguished by their headgear – bowlers and homburgs versus flat-caps. However, all would no doubt sit down to a celebration meal afterwards.

Opposite below: Mrs Bate, the boat-owner's wife, breaks a bottle of champagne on the bow of the Mersey flat *Ruth Bate* in traditional fashion on 18 May 1953, while her husband looks on. Jack Abel (in the trilby) was the owner of the shipyard. This was the last of this type of barge ever built. There is a picture of the *Ruth Bate* being broken up in 1999 in chapter five.

CHAPTER TWO

WOODEN WALLS

The 'wooden walls' of Great Britain were the large wooden sailing battleships of the Royal Navy. They were the principal bulwark and protection against the French – the nation's main continental rival in the eighteenth century. Their protecting role culminated with the Battle of Trafalgar on 21 October 1805, when Admiral Lord Nelson, that most charismatic of naval heroes, won a complete victory over the combined French and Spanish fleets. This victory removed any threat of a French invasion and set the foundations for unchallenged British naval supremacy for the rest of the nineteenth century. Poor Nelson lost his life during the battle, but this 'martyrdom' enthroned him as the patron saint of the Royal Navy and to this day there are Trafalgar dinners at which the toast to his 'immortal memory' is drunk. Nelson's flagship in the battle, HMS *Victory*, is still the flagship of the Royal Navy and is lovingly preserved in dry dock at Portsmouth. If you go on board it today, you cannot help but be impressed by the sheer size of the timbers and the complex construction of its hull and rigging.

A line of battleship like the *Victory* and the smaller frigates like HMS *Trincomalee* (which is still afloat) took vast amounts of English oak and many man hours to build. They were therefore valuable national assets that had to be carefully maintained. Like any other wooden ship, however well built, they were subject to rot and the attack of marine boring worms. At the same time, not so many were needed to be active and sailing in times of peace as in war, so in peace time most ships were laid up 'in ordinary'. In war, it was likely that a few ships remained 'in ordinary' because they were of outdated design or because there were simply not enough men to crew them. In 1784, for example, after the end of the American War of Independence, there were 243 ships laid up 'in ordinary' and 159 in commission. When the Peace of Amiens was signed with France in 1801, there were only eighty-one ships 'in ordinary' out of a total of 945. Laying a ship up in this way was a well-organised process. The ships were kept on safe moorings close to the main dockyards such as Chatham, Portsmouth and Plymouth. All their stores and guns would be removed and the upper masts, spars and running rigging taken into storage. A temporary roof was built over the main deck as protection.

HMS *Hastings* lying at Sheerness in ordinary in 1828. It was a seventy-four-gun ship built at Bombay in 1818 which eventually ended as a stationary guard ship on the Mersey. Note the temporary wooden roof over the main deck.

Lord Newborough's steam yacht the *Vesta* of 1848 was laid up after the summer cruise at its base at Belan Fort, near Caernarfon. Its laying up was along naval lines with all the rigging and spars removed and a temporary pitched roof installed.

HMS *Unicorn*, a sailing frigate, was launched at Chatham in 1824 and immediately placed in ordinary. It was never commissioned and ended up at a Royal Naval Reserve base at Dundee where it still survives afloat with the original roof structure.

One of the two sheer hulks stationed at Portsmouth in the 1820s. Unlike today's floating cranes, this one was permanently moored and ships requiring its service were brought alongside – hence the heavy fendering built out from the hull. Just to the left of the lifting sheerlegs a smoking chimney is visible. It is not clear whether this is for the galley or for a steam winch which could do the lifting instead of men heaving round two capstans.

A skeleton crew would be left on board to keep the vessel secure and work parties from the dockyard made regular visits to carry out maintenance and to pump out any water that had accumulated in the bilges.

Some ships never came out of 'ordinary' because they were too old or there was no call for them. Nevertheless these hulks of wooden walls were still of considerable value to the Navy.

Every dockyard had several for different purposes. Receiving ships accommodated sailors who had just been recruited and the crews of ships that were in dry dock for maintenance. There were prison ships in time of war to house prisoners of war; hulks were not only cheap and available, but they were more difficult to desert or escape from.

There might be a hospital ship if there were no medical facilities ashore, while ships could also be used as store ships to supplement the warehouses ashore. There was even a specialised dockyard support vessel, the sheer hulk, which was the forerunner of the floating crane. The sheer hulk was a line of battleship that had been cut down to one of its lower decks. The main mast was retained and equipped with lifting equipment – the sheers – and these were used for lifting the lower masts of a ship in or out. The lifting tackle was powered by two capstans and the sheer hulk's crew of eight was probably supplemented by other sailors for heavy lifts. Every dockyard had one and there were two at each of the three main dockyards – Chatham, Portsmouth and Plymouth. After the end of the Napoleonic Wars in 1815, the Navy rapidly demobilised. Out of almost a thousand ships, only 368 were left in commission by the end of the year and that latter number kept reducing as the naval budget was progressively reduced. This meant a large number of vessels were either laid up, kept for further use as hulks, or broken up.

The most notorious reuse of discarded warships was as prison ships. The British system of criminal justice in the eighteenth and early nineteenth centuries imposed heavy sentences on the guilty. At the same time the local prisons, many of which dated back hundreds of years, could not cope.

Convicts serving long sentences had been shipped to the American colonies but this outlet was stopped by the Americans gaining their independence. Captain Cook's exploration of the Australian coastline showed (among other things) the potential for establishing a penal colony on the East Coast and this was followed by the first convict settlement at Sydney Cove in 1788. The organisation for transporting those assigned to serve their sentence overseas required holding depots where prisoners sentenced in local courts could be brought together for shipment.

Opposite above: HMS *York* was a prison hulk in Portsmouth Harbour and is seen here taking in another batch of convicts who have been rowed out under heavy guard. The gunports of all three gun decks have been fitted with windows and the lavatories ('the heads') over the bow have been extended. Another hulk can be glimpsed to the right of the *York*'s bow and this probably served as a hospital. Hygiene was of prime importance on the overcrowded decks and this is reflected in the large quantity of washing hanging to dry in the rigging.

Opposite below: The *Discovery* was a Whitby collier barque designed to carry coal from the coal mines of the North East to London. It was purchased by the Admiralty to accompany the *Resolution* for Captain Cook's third voyage of exploration to the Pacific in 1777. Cook was killed in 1778 but the expedition continued under Captain Clarke, the commander of the *Discovery*. Poor Clarke himself also died, but both ships were returned to England in 1780. The *Discovery* became a prison hulk at Deptford Dockyard about 1824. At 300 tons it was much smaller and more overcrowded than the hulks that had been converted from sailing battleships such as HMS *York*.

Wooden warships already performed this function for naval malefactors and it was not difficult to use the same type of accommodation for civilians. HMS *York* was established as a convict ship at Gosport in 1820 and was followed by others moored close to naval bases on the Thames and Medway. One of Captain Cook's exploration ships, the *Discovery*, was berthed at Deptford Dockyard on the Thames and the convicts jailed on board were set to work in the dockyard or on river wall repairs. They were kept under strict escort and their regime on board was very harsh as well. They rose at 5.30 a.m. and, after scrubbing the decks and breakfast, they were taken off to work, returning for dinner at 12.00 noon and then back to work until 5.45 p.m. There were frequent outbreaks of violence, attacks on the guards and attempted escapes. Some hulks were controlled quite loosely and visitors, including females and alcohol, were allowed on board. The overcrowding, lack of hygiene, damp and poor diet predisposed their unfortunate inmates to diseases such as cholera and typhus. In fact, the hulks had a terrible reputation and their inmates were considered to be the lowest dregs of humanity. Those memorable opening chapters of Charles Dickens' novel *Great Expectations* brings out the fear that the hulks evoked and the hero, young Pip, is threatened with being sent to the hulks by his termagant sister:

> *'I wonder who's put into prison ships and why they're put there?' said I, in a general way, and with quiet desperation.*
>
> *It was too much for Mrs Joe, who immediately rose. 'I tell you what, young fellow', said she, 'I didn't bring you up by hand to badger people's lives out. It would be blame to me and not praise, if I did. People are put in the Hulks because they murder, and because they rob, and forge, and do all sorts of bad: and they always begin by asking questions. Now, get you along to bed.'*

By the 1840s the hulks were something of a public scandal and attempts were made to reform them. Some of the worst ones were closed and others improved. Nevertheless these measures did not prevent a mutiny on the *York* in 1848 when a guard was murdered. There was a major riot on the nearby *Stirling Castle* in 1850 and this led to its closure. By 1857, the last of the prison hulks – the *Defence* – was closed, bringing to an end a thoroughly discreditable era in British prison history.

In fact it was not the end of the story, because prison hulks were resurrected shortly after the closure of the *Defence* in an amended form as a reformatory ship for boys. The Youthful Offender's Act of 1854 recognised that juvenile delinquency was a national problem especially in the booming new urban areas. Lawbreakers under the age of sixteen had to be punished separately. The Act became the baseline from which various voluntary charitable organisations were set up to run reform schools to educate, train in an industrial skill and inculcate piety. Pupils had not necessarily broken the law but were 'street urchins' who were at risk of falling into criminal ways. The Liverpool Juvenile Reformatory Association was established in 1856. It was supported by the leading figures in the city including the Earl of Derby and fourteen ship-owners. The Association started three schools: two farm schools and a floating one for training future seamen. The regime, in today's jargon, was to be one of 'tough love'. William Rathbone, the chairman, proposed that 'the boys could expect hard labour, hard fare and a hard bed; treatment must be fair and discipline strict but directed mainly towards deterrence. So might moral reformation come through tempering punishment. The children would be educated to a reasonable standard, given an industrial training and taught there was a God, a heaven and a hell'. The Association obtained the old warship *Akbar* for their work. It had been built of teak in 1801 in Bombay as an East Indiaman and was bought by the Navy for service as a thirty-eight-gun frigate with the name HMS *Cornwallis*. The name was changed to *Akbar* in 1811 when the first name was bestowed on a new seventy-four-gun ship of the line. The *Akbar* was then converted into a troopship to carry reinforcements to Canada during the war of 1812 and afterwards it was hulked for harbour service, first as a hospital ship at Milford Haven and later as a quarantine vessel on the Mersey. Any incoming mariners who were suspected of suffering from the bubonic plague or other infectious diseases had to be isolated for a period before they were allowed ashore. The *Akbar* served the Association until 1862. Its long career demonstrates the continuing value of wooden warships after they had passed beyond active service. The Association's initial intake was of fifty boys, and a local newspaper report in 1857 stated that they had got into 'good trim' and that they 'have learned their duty, learned to respect their officers, to submit to discipline, which is very strict, and have – which is most important of all, for it involves everything else – learned to control themselves, and to stifle or keep under those outbursts of temper which so strongly mark the class from which they spring …' The boys' regime was harsh and monotonous. They slept in hammocks and the day began with stowing these at 5.45 a.m. in the summer and two hours later in the winter. Breakfast was a pint of porridge and four ounces of ship's biscuit. The decks were scrubbed daily and then lessons, mainly in seamanship, occupied most of the day. Dinner consisted of either salt beef or salt pork with either ship's biscuits, potatoes or rice, while on Saturdays there was plum duff (suet pudding with a few raisins) instead of the potatoes. Supper was either a pint of porridge or a pint of coffee. This diet was based on the Board of Trade's regulations for victualling merchant ships and it continued without variation throughout the year. Hygiene on the closely packed decks was regarded as very important and clothing, which was nearly all made on board, was washed on Tuesdays and Fridays, while on Thursdays the boys endured a bath in tepid water. You wonder if the ship was ever really dry, for there was little or no heating aboard and it was not surprising that some of the inmates died. However the experiment was deemed a success and a second, larger *Akbar* was borrowed from the Navy in 1862. It was a seventy-four-gun vessel launched in 1816 at Deptford as HMS *Wellington*. After launching, it spent thirty-two years laid up and from 1848 acted as a depot ship at Sheerness and became flagship and guard ship at Devonport in 1861. Finally it was towed round to Liverpool in May 1862. It was fitted out with a set of masts and yards which were smaller than those for active service and these were used to train the boys in rigging maintenance and to give them confidence when going aloft. The *Akbar* continued to perform its role until 1907. By then it was over ninety years old and its timbers were deteriorating; also, there had been a series

The *Impregnable* training establishment was at based at Devonport Dockyard, Plymouth. It housed and trained new recruits to the Royal Navy. The three-decker on the right accommodated the training facilities which included provision for trainee ratings to learn how to set and furl sails as late as 1912.

of illnesses on board in previous years. Sickness on board, especially respiratory diseases, was common and this in part was the fault of the harsh way of life. As an HM Inspector stated when reviewing the *Clarence* – a Catholic reformatory ship – in 1897: 'I do not believe that death would reap such a harvest from pneumonia if funds allowed more liberal clothing and more sustaining food'. The governing committee for the *Akbar* came to a similar conclusion in 1907. They decided to relocate their school ashore at Heswall on the Wirral, where it continued until 1956. By 1874 seven reformatory ships were in service at various ports. For example, the *Mars* – an eighty-gun ship of 1840 – was stationed off Dundee from 1868 to 1929. The *Mars* had as strict a regime as the *Akbar* and naughty boys in Dundee were admonished with the threat: 'Ye'll get sent tae the *Mars*!'

Wooden warships were also converted for educating boys who were not delinquents. The Royal Navy, in addition to using them as receiving, depot and guard ships also found them useful for accommodating training establishments. HMS *Impregnable* consisted of three converted warships linked together. They provided accommodation and initial training for ratings at Portsmouth. There was a similar establishment for officers at Dartmouth based on HMS *Britannia* and another hulk. The *Britannia* was one of the last wooden warships for the Royal Navy. Launched in 1860 as a 131-gun three-decker, it was fitted with an auxiliary steam engine, but was almost obsolete by the time it was commissioned. After only eight years *Britannia*'s engines and armaments were removed and it became the stationary officer's training ship HMS *Britannia*.

HMS *Eaglet* was the Royal Naval Reserve drill ship at Liverpool from 1862 until 1926 and was tucked away in Salthouse Dock. This was the second oldest dock in the port and by the 1900s its use was confined to coasters and deep-sea sailing ships loading cargoes of Cheshire salt. A steel, full-rigged ship awaiting a cargo can be seen behind the *Eaglet*. The Royal Naval Reserve have a base ashore at Liverpool today and still retain the name and the figurehead from the old ship.

It remained in regular service until 1905 and the future King George V completed his training there. The Britannia Naval College moved ashore but retained the ship until 1916 when it was sent for breaking up. Its departure aroused considerable dismay locally, where it had been such a fixture, and in 1915 there were moves to set up an appeal fund to preserve it. This must be among the first attempts (other than HMS *Victory*) to save a wooden warship for posterity. Needless to say the appeal failed because the nation was in the midst of the First World War.

Wooden warships were also used for training naval reservists. Volunteers with seafaring experience had been recruited as part of the anti-invasion preparations during the Napoleonic Wars, but the Sea Fencibles had been stood down as the French threat receded. The idea was revived in 1853 as the Royal Naval Coast Volunteers, but with few resources and little official encouragement it was not very successful and was wound up in 1873. In 1860, a Royal Naval Reserve was created which recruited from former naval personnel and in the following year it was opened to serving merchant seamen as well. Three drill ships were established at London, Liverpool and North Shields. HMS *Eagle* arrived at the Liverpool depot in 1862. It had been built on the Kentish bank of the Thames at Northfleet in 1804 as a third-rate, seventy-four-gun battleship. It served at sea during the Napoleonic Wars, including taking part in the disastrous Walcheren Expedition in 1809, was rebuilt in 1830 and put back into active service on the South Eastern naval station of South America until 1848. After that it became a coastguard depot ship at various places until final transfer to Liverpool.

Until 1873, when the Royal Naval Artillery Volunteers were formed and opened to young civilians who had interest in naval matters, volunteers had to be professional seamen or fishermen. This proved popular and the Liverpool brigade, which had batteries stationed across the district, numbered nearly 500 men by 1876. Their headquarters was HMS *Eaglet* until the Lords of the Admiralty saw fit to disband them in 1892. In 1903 their successor body, the Royal Naval Volunteer Reserve, was set up and based on the *Eagle* and similar drill ships around the main ports of the country. HMS *Eaglet* (the name was changed in 1918 to allow the *Eagle* name to be transferred to a new aircraft carrier) survived in this role until 1926. Having been afloat for 125 years it was in a poor state, though there was a suggestionthat it would make 'an admirable shipping museum'! After a farewell parade on 2 September, HMS *Eaglet* was stripped of its roof and all the internal fittings in February 1927 and the bare hull was towed away for breaking up. As these old wooden naval depots were withdrawn, they were replaced with equally obsolete or surplus steel warships. The London Naval Reservists, for example, were given HMS *Saxifrage* (renamed HMS *President*), a First World War convoy escort built in 1917. The Belfast Division received HMS *Caroline*, a light cruiser built in 1914 which took part in the Battle of Jutland in 1916 and which continues to serve as their base.

After the end of the Napoleonic Wars, the Royal Navy had more than enough ships laid up in reserve for its own needs and could afford to lend hulks to other organisations. The reformatory movement has already been mentioned and there

The Sloyne anchorage on the south side of the Mersey had berths for four school ships. Two, *Akbar* and *Clarence*, were reformatories, the *Indefatigable* was for orphans and the *Conway* was for training Merchant Navy officers. This shows the *Conway* and the *Akbar*, while the others are obscured by the sails of the yacht belonging to the Royal Mersey Yacht Club which also had its moorings in the Sloyne.

were other charitable organisations which made use of wooden walls. In the early nineteenth century there was no state-funded social service or educational system and help for those in need was organised largely through voluntary societies. The Marine Society was founded in 1756 by Jonas Hanway, a Commissioner on the Victualling Board of the Navy, to support homeless boys in starting a career at sea. The Society established a training ship (an old warship called *Warspite*) in 1786. The Society continues their educational work to this day but now with short training courses for secondary school children and young adults of all backgrounds on their training ship *Jonas Hanway*, which has been converted from a wooden naval minesweeper. Lord Salisbury, the great Victorian social reformer who did so much to gain legislation to improve the working conditions of women and children, also founded a floating orphanage on the frigate *Arethusa* – the last sailing warship to go into action. By 1932, it become too rotten for further use and was discarded in favour of a fine 3,000-ton, steel, four-masted barque, the *Peking*, built at Hamburg in 1911. By 1975, this second *Arethusa* had become too difficult to maintain and the Shaftesbury Society were able to sell this rare survivor to the South Street Seaport Museum of New York. The efficacy of caring for and training poor boys afloat was received wisdom, to the extent that when the London County Council built the new training ship *Exmouth* for orphans in 1904 it was fashioned from steel plates, but still in the shape and with the masts and paint scheme of a wooden warship.

The *Akbar*, the Protestant reformatory ship, retained its appearance as a seventy-four-gun ship with broad white bands along the gun decks and its figurehead intact. The upper masts and the bowsprit have been shortened and there were upper and lower topsail yards which it would not have had when in naval service. These were probably installed to allow the inmates to learn merchant ship practice including setting and reefing sails.

The training ships HMS *Conway* and HMS *Worcester* were also based on old wooden warships. Unlike the floating reformatories or orphanages which trained their charges to be naval ratings or merchant seamen, they aimed to turn out future officers for the Merchant Navy. Their fees made their places only available to boys from well-off families and they were the maritime equivalent of a public school. The *Conway* was established on a converted frigate in 1859 moored in the Mersey and the *Worcester* followed in the Thames in 1862. The Merchant Navy, or rather the Mercantile Marine as it was known then, did not have the coherence of the Royal Navy. It comprised hundreds of companies and individual ship-owners who on the whole were averse to any kind of government interference or legislation. Training for mates and masters of merchant ships had traditionally been a case of being apprenticed to a shipping firm and learning on the job. The introduction of compulsory certificates for competency for merchant officers in 1854 underlined the need for a more systematic way of training future officers. This was recognised by the Mercantile Marine Service Association which was a professional association for master mariners and it was this body who established HMS *Conway*. The original frigate was replaced by the sixty-gun HMS *Winchester* and by 1862 there were 102 cadets on board. It in turn was replaced by the ninety-one-gun battleship HMS *Nile* in 1876. Conditions on board were almost as harsh as the reformatories and there was much bullying by the seniors. In April 1873,

The *Indefatigable* school ship was established by William Clint, a local ship-owner who persuaded the Admiralty to lend him the almost new fifty-five-gun frigate of 1848. He also persuaded James J. Bibby, another ship-owner, to subscribe £5,000 for its conversion. The *Indefatigable* lasted until 1914 when it was replaced by an obsolete steam cruiser. The figurehead survives and is on display in the Merseyside Maritime Museum.

an inspection found that the juniors were not getting sufficient to eat because the seniors always took the lion's share and after that unlimited supplies of bread were issued to them! The new *Conway* proved a sound replacement and was still training boys for a sea career in 1952. By then, it was based in the Menai Straits rather than the Mersey. On 14 April 1952, it was being towed from its mooring at Plas Newydd to the Mersey for a routine dry docking. After taking charge of its two tugs in the violent eddies of the Straits, it went aground. The *Conway* could not be salvaged and in the course of being dismantled in 1956 it was set on fire and burned to the waterline. Many relics of the *Conway*, the *Worcester* and other wooden walls survived into a time when the means for preservation was available. For example, two of the anchors from the *Conway* have been preserved as well as the mizzen mast and two of the rowing gigs, and it and the other training ships also maintain thriving old boys' associations that preserve the memory of these wooden walls.

The spiritual welfare of sailors became a matter of concern to various religious denominations at the start of the nineteenth century. Societies sprang up in ports to raise money to provide bibles for seamen and this work was extended to provide places of worship, usually churches or chapels ashore. In 1819 the Baptist minister Reverend G.C. Smith procured the first floating chapel for sailors on the Thames, the frigate HMS *Speedy*. With its end-to-end roof, it was soon nicknamed 'the Ark'.

H.M.S. "Conway."

Above and left: HMS *Conway* was one of the few 'wooden walls' that survived the Second World War along with the *Foudroyant*, the *Mercury* and the *Implacable* at Portsmouth. The *Conway* was unluckily lost in 1952 and shortly afterwards the *Implacable*, which had been the French flagship *Duguay Trouin* at the Battle of Trafalgar, was taken out and scuttled by the Navy. The *Foudroyant* and the *Mercury* (now back to their original names of *Trincomalee* and *Gannet*) have both been preserved. The photograph shows the *Conway*'s cadets on deck and in the rigging and the ship dressed overall. The occasion was probably the annual rowing match against the cadets of HMS *Worcester*, a training ship on the Thames, which was always keenly contested.

Opposite below: HMS *Caroline* is a light cruiser of 3,750 tons that was built in a record eleven months in 1914. It served with the Grand Fleet and took part in the Battle of Jutland in 1916. It was converted into a drill ship for the Belfast Division of the Royal Naval Reserve in 1926 and continues to perform this role today. Although it has been stripped of its armament, many of the original fittings are still in place, including the steam turbines that were once capable of driving it at 30 knots.

CADET SCHOOL SHIP

H.M.S.
"CONWAY"

(Moored in the Menai Straits)

Training Afloat

RECOGNISED AS A PUBLIC SCHOOL

The " CONWAY " course is planned to fit boys for ultimate command in the M.N. Two years in " CONWAY ", together with the " Conway " Certificate is accepted by the Ministry of Transport as one year's sea service towards qualifying time for 2nd Mate Certificate of Competency Examination. Physical fitness and training receive special attention. Age of admission—between 13½ and 16½ years.

FEES:—*£200 p.a. (including cost of uniform). Reductions for M.M.S.A. and N.E.O.U. members.*

PROSPECTUS FROM:—*Offices, Nautilus House, 6 Rumford Place, Liverpool 3. Secretary : Alfred Wilson.*

Above: HMS *Conway*, as this 1949 advertisement indicates, trained 'cadets' rather than 'boys' and indeed many of its old boys rose to become masters and senior managers in the Merchant Navy. After the loss of the ship, the school moved ashore at Plas Newydd, Anglesey but retained its nautical ethos until it was closed in 1974.

Non-conformists in other ports soon followed. The two-decked, seventy-four-gun HMS *William* built at Liverpool in 1775 became that port's floating chapel in 1820 and another was dedicated at Bristol on 29 August 1821. By 1825, Church of England supporters were planning floating churches in London and Liverpool. HMS *Tees* was opened in Liverpool in 1826 in Georges Dock right in the centre of the port. It was fitted out with a clerestory roof and windows in its gunports, which made the interior light and airy, and there were benches on the gun deck and in a gallery to seat a thousand people. The first chaplain was Dr William Scoresby, who had once been the captain of a Whitby whaling ship and was someone who could preach to sailors on their own terms. The *Tees* lasted until 1872, when it quietly sank at its berth on 7 June. By then, there were many alternatives ashore and congregations had dwindled.

CHAPTER THREE

HULKS

It is worth examining the origins of the word hulk. Today, a modern dictionary defines it as: 'The empty hull of a ship that has been wrecked or cannot be sailed'. This idea is reinforced by Charles Dibdin's famous eighteenth-century sea song 'Tom Bowling', which is sung at the Last Night of the Proms. The first lines are: 'Here, a sheer hulk, lies Tom Bowling/The darling of our crew'. If you look 'hulk' up in one of the older marine dictionaries such as Falconer's of 1769, you will find something similar: 'The name bestowed on any old vessel laid by, as unfit for further service'. It is added that the word was probably derived from the ancient Greek for a cargo vessel. Falconer was right to suggest that it was an ancient term for a cargo vessel but wrong to give it a Greek origin. In fact, it comes from the Anglo-Saxon *hulc* or *holc*, meaning a hollow, and applied to a husk of corn or a peapod, which a ship called a hulk rather resembled, with its curved hull and upturned ends. We can tell from contemporary records that it was widely used around the North Sea and the English Channel and that it may have been in common use as early as the second half of the eighth century. The medieval port of Shoreham, Sussex was actually known as Hulkesmouth, but the main evidence for the appearance of the hulk was its depiction on coins, coats of arms and seals. It is clear from the many surviving examples that the hulk was a large sea-going cargo ship with a single sail. Later examples were fitted with rudders instead of steering oars and had castle-like structures at the bow and the stern. There is even one painting in Sweden which depicts a sixteenth-century hulk with three masts. So, the hulk was once a common and long-lived design of vessel which went to sea and was not permanently moored. The trouble is that we cannot go much beyond this. There have been some very good reconstructions of how a hulk might have been put together; but no one can be sure until the remains of an actual vessel have been found. The mysterious hulk does not seem to have had an 'afterlife' as a wreck or as an abandoned derelict or even in broken-up fragments. Marine archaeology has made much progress since the Second World War and hundreds of medieval wrecks have been found and excavated, but none of them has proved to be a hulk and quite how the name got handed on to stationary storage ships is another mystery.

The hulk or hulc is a medieval mystery. It is known through documents and through many illustrations on seals, manuscripts and carvings, but its construction details are unclear. So far, no one has found a wreck of one to excavate. Hulk pictures date from the twelfth to the sixteenth century, and this painting on glass is based on an oil painting of 1588. It is supposed to show the building of Noah's Ark but it has the characteristics of a hulk which had a full bow and a lot of sheer (curvature in the top planking). Whether it was to be planked in reverse clinker cannot be seen. This type of planking had the strakes overlapping upwards instead of downwards as in most clinker boats. It seems to have been another characteristic of the hulk.

Storage hulks are particularly useful where port facilities are minimal or non-existent. They can provide a ready-made warehouse or store that can be moved if necessary. They can also be used for other purposes where there are not enough facilities ashore. They can house machinery for processing a particular product or they can be used for activities or materials that are better kept away from centres of population, such as the storage of explosives or the isolation of patients with contagious diseases.

One of the factors which contributed to the rapid increase of steamers on the long-distance trade routes was the availability of bunkering facilities. By the late 1860s the adoption of the compound engine supplied with steam from high-pressure boilers had made steamers sufficiently economical to compete with sailing ships for the prime trades to India, the Far East and Australia. But even with the opening of the Suez Canal in 1869, they could not steam all the way without fresh supplies of coal. Many ports may have had access to supplies to local coal but it might not have been suitable. Inferior soft coal also took more space in the storage bunkers. Hard Welsh anthracite was deemed to be the best in the world for firing steamers' boilers. As a result it was considered economical to transport thousands of tons from Cardiff and the other ports of South Wales to coaling stations across the world. In many places where quay storage space was limited it was easier to store the 'black diamonds' in storage hulks anchored offshore. The steamer requiring new supplies might either come alongside the hulk or it might be taken from the hulk to the steamer in barges. The coal hulk was often an old sailing vessel with its masts and sails shorn off. They included ships that had been notable for their speed in their heyday. For example the *Light Brigade*, which ended its days as a coal hulk at Gibraltar, had once been one of the finest ships of the Liverpool–Australia Black Ball Line. The line had been established to capitalise on the demand for passage to the newly found gold fields of New South Wales in 1852. It had built up a reputation for speedy and reliable passages using large American clipper ships. The threat of the American Confederate sea raiders (such as the *Alabama*) caused many Northern ship-owners to sell off their ships cheaply and the Black Ball Line snapped up some prime specimens in 1863, including the *Ocean Telegraph*. This 1,214-ton full-rigged ship had been built in 1854 and had a good reputation for fast voyages between New York and California. Renamed *Light Brigade* (presumably in memory of that tragic charge in the Crimean War), it was placed on the firm's new service from London to Queensland. It also earned them good money as a troopship carrying soldiers out to New Zealand to fight the Maoris. Sold in 1871, it continued trading until 1883 when a Lloyd's surveyor declared it not worth repairing after arriving at Cork with a bad leak. However, it was sound enough to be sold for use as a coal hulk in Gibraltar and was broken up some time before the First World War. The *Light Brigade*'s story is typical of the way ships ended as hulks: they were old, they suffered damage that was not worth repairing for further trading, but they were sufficiently sound to stay afloat as a storage hulk. This humble role might also be allotted to the prime ships of the Royal Navy in old age. HMS *Warrior*, which revolutionised battleship design when completed in 1860, became a stationary training ship, a workshop and then in 1929 a refuelling depot at Milford Haven. In more recent times older tankers have been converted into stores for crude oil. Their use has increased because they can be used to help exploit marginal oil fields or oil fields which are in politically unstable areas. Being afloat and usually away from the centres of population guarantees continuity of production and the safety of their crews. Many have also been equipped with the processing facilities of a production platform and the more recent ones have been built from new rather than being converted from an ageing tanker.

Hulks were used to store all kinds of dry goods as well. Millers liked to have a store of grain in hand to ensure they made their production schedules and to guard against rises in price. Sometimes it was not possible to store all the grain they had purchased

Old tankers can be used for storing crude oil rather than transporting it. Most modern vessels are subjected to rigorous and therefore costly surveys after fifteen years and many are scrapped after twenty years. But some have been converted for storage and processing. This role is especially important in parts of the world where there is an unstable political situation. The steel work welded on the bow of this Norwegian storage tanker at Stavanger carries the pipe work for moving the oil from the well head on the sea.

at the mills and supplementary space was found by hiring barges or hulks. The barges themselves were in effect hulks, that is sailing or steamships that had been converted. The last commercial deep-sea sailing ships survived into the 1930s on one main cargo – grain from South Australia for Europe. They were a cheap method of transport from an area without proper port facilities and they were also floating warehouses which could be directed to the mills which needed their cargo.

More explosive commodities might also be stored in hulks. In 1887, for example, the Liverpool Magazines Co. was founded to take over the storage of explosives. Large quantities of gunpowder were exported to West and South Africa. The company bought three hulks to store this stock and moored them at Bromborough in a remote part of the Mersey. Sailing barges were used to transport small consignments to these ships, which were anchored in the outer estuary well away from the docks. The last of three, the *Swallow*, which had once been a river gunboat, was only scrapped in 1946.

Hulks were important when there was an urgent need for storage and accommodation in remote places. The *Edwin Fox* was built in 1853 in India as a three-masted, full-rigged sailing ship of 747 tons. It spent much of the 1850s as a troopship and afterwards sailed in the Australian and New Zealand trades. In 1885 it was fitted out with a freezing plant for the growing meat trade and used at various ports.

It became redundant as shore plants were completed and ended up being converted into a coal hulk at Picton on the north point of the South Island, continuing to perform this humble role until the 1950s. It has been preserved as a remarkable survivor. The wooden sailing ship with the wonderful name *Glory of the Seas* ended as a cold store for fish at Tacoma, Washington. When its cold store was closed, the *Glory* was deliberately burned so that its valuable copper fittings could be recovered.

South Georgia Island at the southern end of the Atlantic Ocean was even more remote. Over the nineteenth century the hunting of whales had switched from the Arctic to the unexploited seas of the Antarctic regions. Harpoon guns and steam-powered whale catchers had increased the potential catch. But the carcasses had to be processed and this meant having either a sheltered base ashore or a ship with all the blubber cookers and other machinery on board. Anton Larsen, a Norwegian who had worked all his life in whaling, set up the first station on the island at Grytviken in 1904. He bought the old American wooden sailing ship *Louise* to carry all the machinery, stores and factory workers from Norway. The ship then served as

The port of Liverpool's gunpowder hulk *Swallow*, converted from an old gunboat, was moored at Bromborough well upstream of the main port. It was stocked and issued consignments of explosives by four Mersey flats which were locally known as 'the powder hoys'. In the years immediately before closure in 1946, they had their sails taken away and were fitted with engines. This is one of the hoys in the foreground with a member of the crew sculling his 'cock boat' across to the *Swallow*.

The full-rigged 1,535-ton iron ship *Bayard* was built by Thomas Vernon of Liverpool in 1864 for L. Young & Co. of the same port. After various changes of ownership, it was bought in 1898 by a Norwegian ship-owner, L. Gundersen of Porsgrund. This was the fate of many British-owned square-riggers at the end of the nineteenth century. The Norwegians could operate this type of vessel with lower costs than the British. In 1911, it was sold for use as a coal hulk to a Norwegian whaling firm, Christoph Nielsen of Larvik, and stationed at Ocean Harbour on South Georgia Island. In the same year, a severe gale tore the *Bayard* away from its moorings and sent it aground, where it remains to this day. It is firmly wedged on a pinnacle rock which is causing a split across the centre of the hull.

living accommodation while the station was being built and then became the coal store for the whale catchers. Larsen's successful enterprise was copied by other whaling firms who also brought in sailing ship hulks as coal stores for bunkering the whale catchers. Today the *Louise* is no more than a pile of rotten, charred timber after having been set on fire after the British reoccupation of the island in 1982. The iron ship *Bayard* at Ocean Harbour, which was built at Liverpool in 1864, is the most intact of three surviving hulks on South Georgia Island. One of the others, *Brutus*, is partially sunk at Husvik whaling station, which was founded in 1911. The *Bayard* can be taken as typical of most sailing ships that have been converted into hulks. Much of the equipment, such as the hand winch (windlass) for handling the anchors, was left on board. The lower masts were also retained because they could be used for mounting derricks to handle the coal in the hold. The same size of hatches was retained and the officer's cabins in the stern were also kept and used by the crew manning the hulk.

But there were more drastic conversions where the hull of a vessel became incorporated into the shore. This could be either to provide accommodation, storage or act as a pier or as a sea defence against the erosion of the land.

The discovery of gold in California in 1849 brought a huge influx of people from the eastern United States. Many prospectors struck it rich and wanted to enjoy their new-found wealth. Vast quantities of luxury goods – anything from cases of champagne to feather mattresses – were shipped out from the factories back east via Cape Horn on fast clipper ships. San Francisco became the port for the Gold Rush and rapidly ran out of covered warehouse space for all these imports. At the same time, ships were being left idle because their crews had deserted to seek their own fortunes in the gold fields inland. These idle hulks were the solution to the building shortage. Local businessmen converted more than 200 vessels in three years. Most were turned into warehouses, others became offices, hotels, a prison and a church. Many were emptied of their ballast and, with added buoyancy from large casks lashed along the length of their hulls, they were winched well inshore. They were stabilised by piles and piers built all round. Eventually this foreshore was reclaimed and some of them were entirely surrounded by dry land. Over 100 went up in flames along with the newly erected wooden buildings in the Great Fire of May 1851. The remains of one, the *Niantic*, survived. The *Niantic* had been built in 1835 at Chatham, Connecticut for the New York merchant firm, Griswold & Co. They placed it in the China trade until the Gold Rush when it ended up in San Francisco in 1849. After being dragged ashore, a pitched roof was built over the main deck with a set of offices perched over the stern. It was let out as a warehouse and importers would hire space on board by the month. There was a variety of goods stored on board when a fire burned it down to the waterline in 1851. When *Niantic* was rediscovered during foundation excavations in 1978, the archaeologists of the San Francisco Maritime Museum recovered over 3,000 finds in five days of rescue excavations. They included dozens of cases of French champagne and the stock of a stationer: books, pencils and pots of ink. The excavators also managed to salvage a cross-section of the ship's timbers and part of its stern and rudder which were still charred at their upper ends from the fire.

This type of floating or beach commercial operation on hulks was found elsewhere as well. West Africa was a notoriously unhealthy place for Europeans. Tropical diseases, especially yellow fever, carried off many, but the rich opportunities – first in the slave trade and then, after its abolition within the British Empire in 1807, in the palm oil trade – attracted many a young entrepreneur. The unhealthy environment was countered by living aboard a ship. A vessel loaded with trade goods from England would arrive at the mouth of one of the estuaries and anchor. The upper masts and spars would be taken down and a 'house' thatched with palm fronds would be erected over the main deck. It could take several months to barter all the goods for barrels of palm oil. From this it was a short step to the use of a hulk permanently moored in a suitable place. An agent and his staff would man the hulk. Their goods were secure from theft and they themselves stood a better chance of surviving the climate.

Between 1850 and 1900 there were over fifty hulks stationed at various places along the delta of the River Niger. Most were in the 500-ton range and built in the 1840s and 1850s. A few, like the *Winefred* or the *Shackamaxon*, were over 1,000 tons.

The *Lady Jocelyn* was built as a very large (for the time) 2,138-ton iron auxiliary steamer in 1852 at Mare's shipyard on the Thames. The owners, the General Screw Steam Shipping Co., used it to extend their services from the Cape of Good Hope to Sri Lanka and Australia. The company ran into financial difficulties and the ship was sold in 1859. It was eventually converted into a sailing ship and in 1882 (like the *Edwin Fox*) became a stationary refrigerated meat store for Shaw Savill. It then became the Shipping Federation's hostel for strike breakers and was scrapped in 1922.

The *Winefred*, at 1,399 tons, was the biggest ship launched into the shallow River Dee at Chester and for part of its career served in the Black Ball Line. The *Shackamaxon*, 1,369 tons, was built in 1851 for the Cope Line to run a regular packet service between Philadelphia and Liverpool. As conditions ashore were improved, these hulks were discarded and left to rot. The Falkland Islands were another distant British colony where hulks were essential for commerce. The main port and capital at Stanley had little storage space ashore in the nineteenth century and depended on floating storage hulks moored in the middle of the harbour to contain coal supplies for refuelling steamers and the islands' wool crop for export. They also served as temporary stores for cargoes of other ships that had arrived at Stanley for repairs. These hulks were usually ships that had arrived there in distress and had been condemned by the local surveyors as too badly damaged for further trading. Over the years these hulks became old and leaky and were beached alongside the shore. Jetties were built out to them and they were fitted with corrugated-iron roofs. Three survived relatively intact until recently – the *Jhelum*, *Charles Cooper* and the *Egeria*. The first two were abandoned in the 1960s, but the *Egeria*, or more accurately its stern half, is still used by the Falkland Islands Co. at their East Jetty to store lubricants and lifting equipment. It was originally a wooden three-masted barque of 1,066 tons, built at St John New Brunswick in 1859. It arrived at Stanley in October 1872, ninety-five days out from London with a cargo of coal and cement for Callao in Chile.

Hulks were also used to provide temporary living accommodation for major building projects or where it was not feasible to provide housing ashore. In the case of the *Lady Jocelyn* it was to provide protection for its residents. The Shipping Federation was an association of British ship-owners who were determined to fight what they termed 'the strike menace'. Their members included the great liner companies such as P&O, Royal Mail, Orient, Shaw Savill and Albion and between them they controlled 6.5 million tons of shipping. There had been an increasing number of strikes by sailors and dock workers in the 1880s and the Federation was intended to counteract this trend. It issued membership cards to seamen without which they could not expect to obtain jobs on their ships. They were also prepared to intervene in industrial disputes by bringing in 'black legs'. They bought three hulks, the *Paris*, the *Ella* and the *Lady Jocelyn*, together with an ocean-going tug and motor launches. These vessels were normally kept on the Thames, but if a major strike broke out they would be towed to the affected port to act as a dormitory and protected base for their strike breakers. The *Lady Jocelyn*, for example, appeared on the Mersey in June 1911 when a strike by seamen escalated into a general dock and transport workers' walkout. The clash was bitter, with the local authority calling in the Army after a violent end to a mass demonstration in the centre of the city. The *Lady Jocelyn* was an unusual ship because when it had been launched into the Thames in 1852 it was fitted with a small steam engine to assist its passages out to Australia. This was unsuccessful and the bankrupt owners sold it to Shaw Savill & Co., who placed it in the New Zealand emigrant trade. The Federation ceded it to the Admiralty in 1914 to act as a depot ship and by 1918 it was only fit for breaking up. The Federation was given a captured German sailing ship, the *Waltraute* (ex-*Arranmore*) which had been used as a depot ship for submarines. The *Waltraute* was renamed the *Vindicatrix* and in 1939, with war imminent, it was towed round from the Thames to Sharpness and converted into a seamanship school for new recruits to the Merchant Navy.

Civil engineering projects at ports have also employed hulks. The establishment of the South Georgia whaling stations from 1904 meant that there was a large influx of workers who needed to be accommodated from the start of the project, and South Georgia had previously been uninhabited. The building of the Manchester Ship Canal was the 1890s equivalent of building the Channel Tunnel one hundred years later. It cost £15 million to complete and employed thousands of navvies, and at least one of the lodgings was an old wooden sailing ship with a wooden shed perched on top which offered beds and 'tea, coffee and cocoa from 5.00 a.m'. Old passenger liners have also been employed. The White Star liner *Germanic* was built for transatlantic service in 1875 and was sold for further trading to Turkish owners in 1909. It eventually ended up as a workers' hostel in Istanbul. The fine Elder Dempster liner *Aureol* suffered a similar fate. It was the last passenger liner to call at

The beautiful *Aureol* was the flagship of the Elder Dempster Line that ran passenger and cargo services from Liverpool to West Africa. Built by Alexander Stephens & Co. at Glasgow in 1951, the 14,000-ton *Aureol* was the last passenger liner to sail regularly from the port of Liverpool. Its last sailing was on 16 March 1972. It was sold to a Greek shipping company who hired it out as an accommodation ship for foreign building workers at the Saudi port of Jeddah until 1979. After another spell as an accommodation ship in the 1980s and a long lay up at Piraeus, the *Aureol* was scrapped.

Liverpool on 16 March 1972. The end of the colonial government with the granting of independence to the West African states along with the invention of the jet aircraft made sea passenger services massively unprofitable. In 1974 the *Aureol* was sold to a Greek firm who sent it to Jeddah, the main port of Saudi Arabia, as a port workers' accommodation ship. Today, there are purpose-built accommodation barges – coastels – run by firms such as the Bibby Group of Liverpool. They have hired their fleet for many purposes, including as a temporary accommodation for Army engineers in the Falklands to acting as floating prisons. Incidentally, they offer a far higher standard of accommodation than the old prison hulks!

Even hulks can have an 'afterlife', because even when they are worn out and cannot be kept afloat or beached in one piece, they can be broken up and their component parts recycled. They can also be used to improve the facilities or safety of a harbour. Hulks have been beached to form landing stages or piers; they were floated into position and then weighted down with rock to ensure they did not float away. The old Cumbrian-built barque the *Vicar of Bray* of 1841 performed this duty at Goose Green in the Falkland Islands and at Punta Arenas, the most southerly port in Chile, two sailing ships and a steamer formed a breakwater to protect the slipways of the local naval base. Hulks have also been sunk offshore. The steel, four-masted barque *Hougomont* of 1897 was dismasted in 1932 while on passage to Australia. Its crew succeeded in sailing it to Adelaide with temporary sails rigged on what remained of its masts, but the Finnish owners could not afford the cost of re-rigging. As a result it was stripped of anything useful and towed out to form a breakwater at Stenhouse Bay. Once in the correct position, a small explosive charge in the hold was detonated and it went down. Small wooden boats and barges have often been used to help support banks against erosion or to stabilise a channel or even just to fill in a redundant dock. Examples can be found all around the British coast, for example at Bradwell, where the mouth of the River Blackwater has a row of steel Thames lighters sunk along the shore as sea defences. On the River Mersey, dozens of local wooden barges (flats) have been sunk to prop up eroding banks or, as at the Big Pool at Runcorn, simply to reclaim an area of water. At Llannerch y Môr on the North Wales coast an old barge, the *Elmarine*, which was built of reinforced concrete in the First World War, was used partly to defend the entrance of this tiny harbour and partly to act as a water reservoir for the leisure enterprise nearby in case of fire.

The concrete barge *Elmarine* dates back to the First World War when a shortage of steel brought about the building of barges, coasters and even ocean-going freighters in reinforced concrete. It was bought by the owners of the *Duke of Lancaster*, a shopping and leisure venture on the north coast of Wales at Llannerch y Môr, and was sunk partly as breakwater and partly to use the hold as a water reservoir in case of fire.

Above: A hulk used as a landing stage, the *Vicar of Bray* provided a landing stage for the settlement at Goose Green in the Falkland Islands. It was used to receive supplies by sea from Stanley and to send away bales of wool. The *Vicar* was a 251-ton, three-masted barque built at Whitehaven, Cumbria in 1841. It put into Stanley in distress in 1871 and was bought by the Falkland Islands Co. They used it to carry cargoes to and from England. When it was no longer fit for sailing, the *Vicar of Bray* was cut down to a storage hulk and eventually taken round to Goose Green for this final use. There was a proposal to salvage and restore it at San Francisco as the last survivor of the Californian Gold Rush, but this has come to nothing.

Top: With little warehousing ashore, floating or beached hulks were a vital part of the Stanley maritime economy. All the hulks have been broken up or abandoned except for the stern section of the *Egeria*. This 900-ton, Canadian-built barque has been built into the Falkland Islands Co. wharf.

Above: The 'tween deck of the *Egeria* is still used to store drums of lubricating oil and cargo-handling equipment. The massive timbering and the corrugated aluminium roof have enabled this last hulk to remain intact. However in recent years the waterline timbers have been attacked by the teredo worm which will eventually lead to it collapse.

Opposite below: Stanley Harbour, the Falkland Islands in 1871. In this, the earliest photograph of shipping at Stanley, there are many sailing ships at anchor undergoing repairs. The *Vicar of Bray* is on the extreme left, then there is a local schooner and then a storage hulk without masts, with HMS *Galatea* beyond it. To the right there are several ships awaiting repair and the beached hulk of the *Actaeon*, which is linked to the land by a pier. The *Actaeon* had a large aperture cut through it to form a loading platform. Goods were stored in it or taken ashore by means of hand-propelled trucks running on a narrow-gauge tramway.

Sunken hulks can be an important resource for maritime archaeologists. The best example might be the rediscovery of a Norfolk keel propping up a bank at Whitlingham on the River Yare in 1985. The Norfolk keel was the predecessor of the better-known Norfolk wherry and had never been recorded before they had all been taken out of service. This was probably the last one afloat, and was hulked as a bank support about 1890.

So though the term 'hulk' has a negative ring to it, hulks have proved exceedingly useful in many ways, from stores to training schools or hostel accommodation, or finally just for preventing land slipping into water.

CHAPTER FOUR

CONVERSIONS: NEW USES FOR OLD SHIPS

We have covered part of this topic in the chapters on wooden walls and hulks, both of which were a form of conversion. The wooden walls were transformed from sailing battleships of the line into floating accommodation for training schoolboys or sailors. Hulks tended to be merchant sailing ships that had had most of their masting and rigging taken down and their cargo holds used for storage. There were also less obvious forms of conversion. One of the most important in the days of steamships was the conversion of marine boilers from coal firing to heavy fuel oil. This led to no obvious outward changes, but it made for a saving in labour by doing away with the 'Black Gang' who shovelled the coal. It also did away with the dirty business of bunkering the ship with coal. There have also been many examples of steamers being converted to diesel ships either to extend their working lives or to reduce costs. This leaves many other new uses for old ships and these can be split into the following categories: conversions for further use at sea, conversions for wartime use, and conversions for leisure or cultural purposes other than restoration as an historic ship, which is dealt with in chapter eight. There have also been quite a lot of ships that have been turned into living accommodation. Finally there is a sub-section of vessels that have been put ashore and turned into buildings.

The most elementary external conversion is a change in use which involves either the adding of extra equipment or the taking away of existing kit to fit the ship for its new purpose. Brunel's ship, the *Great Britain*, is a good example. It was completed in 1843 with a steam engine and a screw propeller as its main propulsion system with auxiliary sails on five masts. The *Great Britain* was intended for a passenger service across the Atlantic from Liverpool to New York. It ran aground in Dundrum Bay, Northern Ireland in October 1846, but was salvaged after a lot of effort and brought back to Liverpool and laid up because it had bankrupted its owners. It was eventually bought in 1850 for a bargain price of £18,000 and was refitted with a smaller auxiliary engine and a large rig on four masts. Additional passenger cabins were also installed on the main deck. This refit enabled it to sail long distances and only rely

The *Great Britain* was converted to an auxiliary sailing ship to enable it to ply on the 13,000-mile voyage from Liverpool to Melbourne. In 1856-57 it was given a three-masted rig with a main yard 105 feet long. The engines drove a single propeller which could be lifted out of the water when not in use. This reduced the drag of the hull when under sails alone.

on the engine when the wind failed. Its new owners, Gibbs Bright, exploited it to the full by putting it on to a new service from Liverpool to Melbourne. There was huge demand for cabins because of the recent discovery of large amounts of gold inland from Melbourne. The *Great Britain* had a second refit in 1857 when it was re-rigged a second time with a conventional three-masted ship rig. It continued to run as an auxiliary to and from Australia until 1875. The hull was still sound but the engines and boilers were worn out. They and all the passenger cabins were removed and it became a bulk-carrying sailing ship. The *Great Britain* was damaged in a Cape Horn gale in 1883 and was condemned as unseaworthy at Stanley in the Falkland Islands and sold for further use as a floating storage hulk. It performed this humble but essential task until beached in Sparrow Creek in 1937, from where it was salvaged for preservation in 1971. The *Great Britain* was not the only early steam liner to be converted into a sailing ship. The Cunard Line's *America* of 1848, *Asia* of 1850 and *Arabia* of 1853 were all built as wooden paddle steamers and were sold for further use under sail alone. The *Asia*, for example, was converted in 1867 and carried cargoes until 1877, when it caught fire at Bombay. On a smaller scale, Lord Newborough's steam yacht the *Vesta* of 1848 was sold in 1873. It had been bought by John Whyte, a Liverpool ship-owner, who removed the engine, boiler, propeller and luxurious accommodation. The *Vesta*'s lofty topsail schooner rig was retained and it became a humble cargo carrier until it disappeared without trace two years later.

In more recent times there have been many more conversions of powered ships into sailing ships due to the fact that there has been a growing interest in sail training and cruising under sail. There have, however, been few opportunities to buy the hulk of an original sailing ship in good condition. Danish, and some of the other Baltic shipbuilders, were still building fine wooden schooners with auxiliary diesel engines after the Second World War. As they came out of commercial service many were bought for conversion for cruising or film work. Squaresail of Charlestown, Cornwall, has three ships employed on film work, corporate hospitality and sail training. The *Phoenix* was built as a schooner for the Danish Evangelical Mission in 1929. In 1991 it was used as Columbus' flagship, the *Santa Maria*, in the film *Columbus* and in 1996 it became a brig of the 1750s era. The *Earl of Pembroke* was a three-masted schooner built in Sweden in 1948 and is now a late eighteenth-century barque which has appeared as a slave ship in the television drama *A Respectable Trade*. The *Kaskalot*, the biggest of the three, has a strong wooden hull used for trading to Greenland in 1948. Rigged as a barque, it made an ideal stand-in for the polar expedition ship *Endurance* in a television documentary drama about Sir Ernest Shackleton. This film, with Kenneth Branagh as Shackleton, was filmed in the *Kaskalot*'s old trading area off the coast of Greenland. Squaresail also train young people in the old sailing ship skills and use them to crew their ships.

Other types of vessels have been turned into sailing ships. Fishing vessels and lightships which both have strongly built hulls of the right shape have been successfully transformed. Greenpeace, the environmental pressure group, owns the schooner *Rainbow Warrior*, which was converted in 1995 from the Norwegian sealing vessel *Arctic Surprise*. The ship had to be bought by stealth with a company set up for the purpose, because the Norwegians would never have allowed Greenpeace to buy it because of their opposition to sealing and whaling. The German sail training ship *Alexander von Humboldt*, built in 1906, was once a lightship off Kiel. Nearer home, the Sobriety Trust – which runs youth training projects and a waterways museum at Goole – wanted a training ship that could represent the old coasting ketches nicknamed 'billy boys'. They all originated from Goole and the inland ports of the Humber, and the last one had been scrapped in the 1960s. They found a worthy substitute in an old Humber lightship which has become the billy boy *Audrey*. Many of the Thames barges which are still sailing today ended up as motor ships in the 1950s. Most had engines fitted after the Second World War and as sails wore out they were not replaced. The diesel engines took up little space – only the poor skipper lost part of his cabin to the engine. But so long as their hulls were sound and there was cargo to be carried they continued to be useful commercial coasters. Some of these original Thames barges, which have been kept sailing long after coming out of trade in the 1960s, are now getting beyond economic repair. Two new barges have been fashioned out of other types of vessels; one was a Thames lighter which was given a new bow and stern and the other was a Dutch motor barge which was shortened. Conversions can go the other way too, with sailing vessels being turned into fully powered ships. The barque *Elissa* of 1877 ended up as a Greek motor coaster before being bought for restoration. During the Second World War, the

German submarine campaign created such a scarcity of tonnage that the *Leyland Brothers* of 1886, which had been a Portuguese hulk since 1912, was converted into the diesel tanker *Nagala* and carried on trading until 1967.

New commercial uses for steamers and motor ships have been extremely varied down the years. Brunel's 'wonder ship' the *Great Eastern* proved to be unsuccessful as a passenger liner and was bought for conversion into a cable-laying ship in 1864. With three large cable tanks installed in the holds and large winches and pulleys at the stern and the bow for laying or recovering cable, it proved to be a very successful conversion. The *Great Eastern* laid the first telegraph cable across the Atlantic in 1866 and went on to lay another four long-distance cables – three across the Atlantic and one from Suez to Bombay. In the 1990s the demand for ocean floor telephone cables has increased in spite of satellite communications and to meet the demand an oil drilling ship was converted into the cable-layer *Nexus* to enable BT to lay extra cables. This was unusual in the sense that it was a vessel from the offshore oil industry that was used; usually the offshore oil firms have converted existing vessels to their purposes. Crude oil storage in old oil tankers has already been mentioned, but there are now whole floating oil and gas processing plants mounted on older hulls. The oil industry has also found work for the many redundant British fishing trawlers. They are used as safety and standby vessels to keep other ships away from production platforms and to evacuate their crews in the event of an emergency. Big trawlers make ideal vessels for this kind of work because they were designed to stay at sea however

The topsail schooner *Julia af Faaborg* was built as a Baltic auxiliary schooner in 1938 and was converted to an older topsail schooner rig in 1968. It is currently owned by the Turk Group and has appeared in the recent *Hornblower* television series along with their replica frigate, the *Grand Turk*.

The *Audrey* was built as a lightship for the Humber estuary. The shape of its hull and its strong build made it ideal for conversion into a replica of a ketch-rigged billy boy. The latter was a bluff-bowed coaster that was particular to Goole and the neighbouring inland ports. There were no surviving billy boys to be preserved.

bad the weather. It was for the same reason that the Falklands government hired two deep-sea stern trawlers from John Marr & Co. of Hull to act as fishery patrol ships in its stormy fishing zone. The sale of fishing licences to Japanese and Korean fishing fleets, which mainly catch squid, is the main source of income for the islands and it has to try to ensure that there is no over-fishing or illegal fishing. Other trawlers owned by the same company have been converted into research and seismic survey vessels, as in the case of the *Cumulus*, a weather ship stationed in the mid-Atlantic.

Other conversions have gone in the opposite direction, where service vessels have been turned into cargo ships. The Liverpool pilot cutters such as the *Earl of Liverpool* of 1835, the *Auspicious* of 1849 and the schooner *Pioneer* of 1852 have all ended up as coasting cargo ships in West Africa. The last Liverpool schooner, the *George Holt* of 1892, was sold to the Falkland Islands Co. for carrying supplies and wool exports round the islands. In similar fashion all four of Liverpool's first steam pilot boats were sold for further work. Three became coasters and the fourth, *Queen Victoria* of 1898, was sold in 1924 and was converted into the motor yacht *Enchantress*. All these vessels were built to a high specification and there was plenty of work left after the Pilot Service decided they were obsolete for their own particular purposes.

Some conversions were so bizarre and specialised as to be hardly credible. The early steamer *Courier* was converted from steam to horsepower in 1818. This was after its sister ship, the *Telegraph*, had burst its boiler at Norwich in 1817. Nine passengers were killed and six seriously injured and the accident led to the setting up of a Parliamentary Select Committee to investigate boiler safety. The owner, Richard Wright, decided to try and hang on to his customers by replacing the boiler and engine with an 18-foot-diameter platform round which four horses walked. They turned an upright shaft which was geared to the paddles. The conversion was apparently a success even though the journey between Norwich and Great Yarmouth was lengthened. In the Second World War, the Royal Navy had a series of small steam coasters for delivering ammunition, water and supplies to warships. They were modelled on the Clyde puffer, with a simplified hull form to assist with prefabrication. Some of these VICs (Victualling Inshore Craft) continued to serve after the war and survived long enough to be taken up either by steam enthusiasts or for further work. VIC 35 was converted into the motor ship *Crazy Diamond of Penzance* and makes a living salvaging scrap from the many wrecks in the area, while at Truro another VIC (number unknown) was used to conduct trials on a new steering system and then became a gatherer of seaweed for a firm that extracted the alginates used in the food industry.

One of the most common conversions for further use was changing a ship from a self-propelled vessel into a dumb barge. The engines and boilers may have worn out or be beyond economic repair. Many sailing ships could not find work or their hull, masts and rigging were no longer fit for sea, but they had sufficient strength to be used for towage in sheltered waters. Many Severn trows, Mersey flats, Humber keels and Thames barges all had their working careers extended by conversion into dumb barges. The particular design of their hulls and their cargo capacities still suited their particular estuaries and waterways. On the Blackwater estuary, Thames barges were shorn of their sails and masts to act as lighters to carry timber from freighters at anchor to Heybridge Basin up to the 1960s. Some trades which did not produce large profits depended on buying old but serviceable vessels and turning them into barges. Abel & Son of Runcorn specialised in dredging sand from the Mersey for the glass industry and for building purposes. Their fleet of barges was a mixture of ex-sailing flats, an ex-topsail schooner, a former lightship and a stripped-out steamer. There are also dumb barges that have been converted for other uses such as workshops and floating repair docks. These conversions can be seen around the Thames estuary, for the decline of the traditional lighterage traffic on the Thames left a surplus of cheap lighters. At Maldon, the Thames Barge Sailing Club has a Thames lighter as a floating workshop for maintaining its two sailing barges, and nearby a lighter has had its bow cut off to form a small floating dock that can take smacks, yachts and Thames barges.

The demands of war call for all kinds of improvisation to sustain the campaign and arguably no more so than at sea. Monarchs have requisitioned merchant ships since the Middle Ages. At that time it was usually a case of providing them with a troop of soldiers and perhaps some temporary fortifications at the bow and the stern.

Since the increasing number of fishing restrictions (for example around Icelandic waters), the British deep-sea trawler fleet has all but disappeared. The older vessels went for scrap but the more modern ships were given new work in the offshore oil industry as safety vessels or, in the case of the of the *Falklands Protector*, as a fishery patrol ship.

The VIC (victualling inshore craft) was a standard Second World War design of small steam coaster modelled on the Clyde puffer. This example was originally a supply vessel for the Navy. It was later converted into a motor vessel and eventually ended as a seaweed gatherer based at Truro, Cornwall.

VIC 32 had a very different conversion; it has been converted into a cruise ship steaming on the Caledonian Canal and to the Western Isles with passenger accommodation in the cargo hold.

The Cunard Line had a reputation for building strong vessels and many went on to further uses. The *Campania*, which had been built in 1893, was converted into a seaplane carrier in the First World War with a launching ramp over its bow. The aircraft were stored below and brought up on deck by a lift.

The *Campania* met its end in 1918 when it was sunk in a collision in the Firth of Forth.

Above: The *Cevic* of 1894 was a cattle carrier in the White Star Line. In 1914, it and a number of other cargo ships were disguised as specific battleships. The 8,330-ton *Cevic* was turned into the 30,000-ton battle cruiser *Queen Mary* and sent to cruise the Atlantic. In 1916 it was converted into a refuelling tanker for the Navy and after the war became a commercial tanker.

Opposite: The New Zealand Steam Ship Co.'s SS *Mamari* underwent one of the most radical conversions and was rebuilt to look like HMS *Hermes,* the aircraft carrier. The effort undertaken to do this involved the removal of much of its superstructure and the building of a flat top. All this, just to pretend to the Germans in 1939 that *Hermes* was somewhere it wasn't.

In later centuries warships became more specialised, while navies also required support from merchant shipping. This was not just for delivering troops and supplies. Some of the largest liners, such as the White liner *Britannic,* were turned into hospital ships to help with the huge number of casualties. In terms of defence, one finds that in both world wars large numbers of fishing trawlers were converted into anti-submarine patrol vessels and paddle steamers, which had hitherto carried holidaymakers, were turned into minesweepers or anti-aircraft vessels.

Small wooden sailing schooners and barges were taken as moored base ships for flying barrage balloons in the Second World War. This inevitably meant that no maintenance was carried out on them and they were in no fit state for further trading at the end of the war. Merchant ships might also take the offensive. Going back to the 1880s, the Admiralty had paid a subsidy to the owners of fast passenger liners which allowed them to be converted into armed merchant cruisers. They were permanently fitted with gun mountings to allow for rapid conversion. Their wartime role was to attack enemy merchant shipping and they relied on their superior speed rather than armour plating to take them away from danger. The converted Cunard liner *Carmania* encountered the *Cap Trafalgar,* its German

equivalent, on its first patrol in September 1914 and sank it. On a smaller scale, the First World War saw the deployment of Q-ships. These were fishing smacks, schooners or small coasters which patrolled as bait for enemy submarines. They all carried a hidden gun disguised behind collapsible bulwarks or deck houses. There were also a small number of larger cargo ships which were carefully disguised as individual British battleships to try and fool the enemy. Other merchantmen were turned into aircraft carriers. A number of the Isle of Man Steam Packet Co.'s ships became seaplane tenders, with cranes to lift their aircraft into or out of the water. The Cunard liner *Campania* of 1893 was due to be scrapped into 1914, but was taken up by the Admiralty and converted into a seaplane carrier with an inclined flight deck from which its ten aircraft could be launched. Merchant aircraft carriers were taken a stage further in the Second World War with the MAC ships. These usually were tankers or bulk carriers which were given a temporary flight deck above their superstructure. They carried a small number of fighters to defend the Atlantic convoys from German air attacks. Later in the war, they deployed Swordfish aircraft carrying depth charges to attack enemy submarines. Improvised aircraft carriers have also be seen in later wars. The Harrison Line's container ship *Astronomer*, for example, was quickly converted into a carrier for helicopters and Harrier jets in the 1982 Falklands War.

A great many ship conversions have been concerned with making vessels into leisure facilities or living accommodation. Cruise ships are now largely purpose built, but when cruising first became fashionable in the 1920s and '30s cruises were undertaken by ordinary passenger liners. Cruising helped the Cunard Line to weather the downturn in Atlantic traffic after the Wall Street Crash of 1929. The same happened in the 1960s as the competition from jet aircraft intensified. By 1962, the Cunard Line was losing money on its regular passenger service and it was therefore decided to convert the *Saxonia* and the *Ivernia* for cruising mainly in the West Indies for the American market. They were both fairly new ships launched in 1954 for the Liverpool service. Their conversion cost £12 million, which was a huge sum then, and it was mainly spent on installing air conditioning and en-suite bathrooms. They were also renamed *Carmania* and *Franconia* and repainted with distinctive light-green hulls. By 1970 their fuel and staff costs were increasing and they were also due for refit. They were laid up and were eventually sold to the Russian Black Sea Shipping Group to continue as budget cruise liners and occasional troopships. At 20,000 tons they were both small compared to today's cruise ships, some of which are in excess of 100,000 tons. Very small ships and canal barges have also been converted for cruising, while another of the VIC coasters, VIC 32, a mere 96 tons and 66 feet long, takes twelve passengers on cruises around the West Coast of Scotland every summer.

Restaurant owners are in fierce competition with their rivals and there is much to be gained by creating novel surroundings. Old ships can offer a distinctive environment because they are on the water. The Thames Embankment enjoys a selection of floating eateries established on some interesting ships. These include the paddle steamer *Tattershall Castle* of 1934, once a Humber ferry, the Clyde excursion

The old White Star liner SS *Runic* was sold at the end of its useful passenger-carrying life to the New Sevilla Whaling Co. and converted into a factory ship. It retained its buff and black funnel but its stern was altered to include a ramp for hauling dead whales up onto the deck for processing. The advent of whale ships like the *New Sevilla* saw an end to the age-old practice of sailing ships being used for whaling.

steamer *Queen Mary II* of 1933 and the *President* of 1918, a naval convoy escort turned firstly into the London Royal Naval Reserve Headquarters and finally into a restaurant. There is also the *Wellington*, a naval sloop of 1934 which acts as the appropriate Livery Hall for the Honourable Company of Master Mariners. You will probably not find a similar collection of ships converted for eating afloat, but there will be at least one at many of the ports where commercial traffic has given way to leisure and waterfront. Quite often they will be a converted Dutch canal barge, such as those at Ipswich and Bristol. With their roomy cargo holds plus a tented area on deck, they can provide plenty of space for their diners and drinkers. All kinds of other vessels have been converted for eating and entertainment, including lightships at Ipswich or Blyth, the latter being the club ship of the Royal Northumbrian Yacht Club. There are also fishing boats, Thames barges and cross-Channel ferries. The *Tuxedo Princess* was a roll-on roll-off ferry dating back to the 1960s and is now moored below the bridges at Newcastle as a huge nightclub. There are, however, many problems with operating leisure facilities on board old ships. Their age means that most of their electrical and ventilating systems are wearing out, or the location may be just too out of the way to attract customers. There can be hazards such as large amounts of asbestos lagging in the engine room, and the local licensing authorities and the fire prevention officer may make expensive demands.

The drifter *Sea Breeze* was acting as a tender to large warships such as the cruiser in the background. It was built in 1918 at Aberdeen and went on to serve in the Second World War, one of hundreds of fishing vessels converted into auxiliary naval vessels.

Old powered ships have been converted into dumb barges. The *Lonsdale* on the right, belonging to Richard Abel of Runcorn, was receiving grain from a deep-sea cargo ship via a floating elevator. It started as the paddle tug *Lord Clive* and was converted in about 1900 and only scrapped in 1966.

This lighter has undergone a more radical conversion into a dry dock. It is widely used for heavy repairs to traditional sailing craft such as this Colchester oyster smack, which has been replanked and awaits redecking and new bulwarks at Maldon, Essex, in 1996.

The *Golden Galleon* was built as a Fairmile class motor launch in 1942 and was equipped with a 3-pounder gun and two machine guns for harbour and estuary patrols. With two petrol engines, it had a top speed of about 20 knots. After the Second World War it was converted into an excursion ship for cruising on the Norfolk Broads with much reduced engine power.

Motor gunboats were designed to attack German E boats in the Second World War. Their main armament was a 2-pounder gun and they had a top speed of about 40 knots. This example was converted into a neat houseboat in the quiet waters of Thorpe near Norwich.

The restaurant ship *Prince Albert* arriving at Canning Dock, Liverpool. This former yacht fell foul of the fire regulations and eventually left after three years of idleness. It was last seen at a ship-breaker's yard at Ipswich.

The 4,972-ton cross-Channel steamer the *Duke of Lancaster* was built in 1956 and in 1978 was bought to be the 'Fun Ship' beached at Llannerch y Môr in the Dee estuary. This was to be partly a shopping centre and partly for eating and entertainments. Unfortunately the scheme fell foul of the regulations and was never fully realised.

At Liverpool, for example, there have been a series of failed ventures. They include Thames barge *Edith May*; the Isle of Man steamer *Manxman*; the *Conway*, a fake wooden warship created out of a trawler; the *Royal Iris*, an ex-Mersey ferry; and the *Prince Albert*, whose owner was employing illegal immigrants from the Ukraine at £1 an hour. Closed club ships have been towed to other ports: the *Manxman* has ended up on the Tyne and the *Royal Iris* on the Thames. Both have failed and their next berth will probably be the breaker's yard.

The performing arts have also made use of converted ships. There is the *Thekla*, a permanently moored coaster in Bristol Docks which is a theatre, while the Walk the Plank Theatre Co. take their shows on tour in a converted Norwegian ferry. On a smaller scale, the Mikron Theatre Co., usually with a cast of four, tour the canals putting on plays in pubs and church halls in a converted narrow boat. Barges have also been turned into floating art galleries and in one instance a book shop. There have been floating exhibition ships such as the *Campania*, which was a Second World War aircraft carrier which carried a Festival of Britain exhibition on tour in 1951, and also floating trade shows such as those that Gestetners mounted on the schooner *Charlotte Rhodes*. Gestetners made duplicating machines in the days before the dominance of the photocopier and in the early 1970s hired the *Charlotte Rhodes* to tour an exhibition of their products around the coast. This was shrewd, because the *Charlotte Rhodes* – yet another conversion from a Baltic schooner – was a television celebrity: it was James Onedin's ship in the Victorian shipowning drama series, *The Onedin Line*.

Left: Dutch barges have been imported into British ports in some numbers for conversion to static floating accommodation or for nightclubs or restaurants. This particular example is a smart restaurant moored in Ipswich Dock on the quay where the last Thames barges used to tie up.

Below: The Bridgewater Canal motor barge *Parfield* of 1952 was used to transport maize from Liverpool Docks to Kellogg's mills in Manchester. This trade finished in 1974 and it was sold for use as a rubbish barge. The *Parfield* was subsequently converted into a floating mobile home but retains its original appearance.

The *Sarah Abbot* was the same type of barge as the *Parfield* and it too has been converted for living accommodation, as *Black Abbot of the Mersey*. Its conversion, with the large saloon covering half the deck, fits in well with the overall shape.

Smaller vessels have also been converted into floating homes. Barges, with their flat bottoms and their capacious single holds, have been popular choices. Quite a number of Thames barges were converted into houseboats after the Second World War when there was a housing shortage around London. In the same era there was also a surplus of small warships such as motor torpedo boats. With their massive engines removed they had ample space below decks. There were whole collections of houseboats in the tidal creeks, including around the Medway and up to the Orwell estuary. Many of these miscellaneous collections have been cleared away as the residents have moved ashore or as the boats have rotted. Pin Mill on the Orwell still has quite a collection which is mixed in with rotting hulks and Thames barges under repair. They include a unique surviving barge from the Gipping Navigation and an ex-naval water carrier. Further up the Orwell you will find Ipswich Dock contains more modern examples of floating accommodation, including a sturdy Scottish fishing boat and a Dutch sailing barge.

A few vessels have also been dragged ashore for conversion to new uses. Fishermen at Brighton cut their old 'hog boats' in two and erected the two halves as storage sheds for nets. Other old boats were used as roofs for sheds and residences. The most famous was the one described by Charles Dickens in *David Copperfield*, Peggotty's house on the sands of Great Yarmouth:

I looked in all directions, as far as I could stare out over the wilderness, and away at the sea, and away at the river, but no house I could make out. There was a black barge or some kind of superannuated boat not far, high and dry on the ground, with a black funnel sticking out of it for a chimney and smoking very cosily: but nothing else in the way of habitation was visible to me.

'That's not it?' said I. 'That ship-looking thing!'

'That's it, Mas'r Davy', returned Ham.

If it had been Aladdin's pale, roc's egg and all, I suppose I could not have been more charmed with the romantic idea of living in it. There was a delightful door cut in the side, and it was roofed in, and there were real windows in it; but the wonderful charm of it was, that it was a real boat which had no doubt been on the water hundreds of times, and which had never been intended to be lived in on dry land.

This was not drawn from Dickens' imagination, for there were indeed old fishing boats used as homes on dry land and one has been preserved at the Fisheries Museum at Esbjerg, Denmark. Vessels on dry land have also been used for other purposes. Small vessels such as lightships and fishing boats have been used as pieces of landscaping sculpture. Breton fishing villages sometimes have an example of their local fishing boat preserved at the entrance to their village. One of the strangest is the Mersey mini-lightship which marks the entrance to the former Fun Ship at Llannerch y Môr on the North Wales coast. The Fun Ship itself was once the Irish Sea ferry *Duke of Lancaster*, which was put ashore on a very high tide, and the lightship no longer advertises the closed Fun Ship but is used by local political campaigners as a billboard.

Opposite above: Surveyor No.1 was one of a flotilla of six motor surveying ships used by the Mersey Docks and Harbour Board to record the depths of water and positions of sandbanks in the Mersey and its approaches. It has been sympathetically converted into a pleasure cruiser. The only changes to the appearance are the white instead of black hull and the mast.

Opposite below: The Walk the Plank Theatre Co. operate this converted Norwegian ferry as a travelling theatre with the stage and audience on the vehicle deck. The paint scheme is based on the design and colours of an Admiralty chart.

Another cultural conversion: the Sobriety Trust (named after a Humber keel and not a Temperance campaign) run their art gallery afloat on a converted keel alongside their maritime museum in Goole Docks.

One of the most notable ships converted into a floating exhibition was the old wooden sailing barque *Success*. Built in 1840 as an ordinary general trader, it was converted into an Australian women's prison in 1860. It later became a boys' reformatory. In 1884 it was sold and converted into an exhibition ship. The new owners toured it under the guise of one of the original convict transport ships that sailed to Australia at the end of the eighteenth century. The exhibits were sensational rather than accurate. The *Success* was sunk, salvaged and sailed for Britain in 1892. It toured extensively and eventually ended up in the USA in the 1930s.

A real example of Peggotty's house described by Charles Dickens in *David Copperfield*. This is on show at the Fisheries Museum at Esbjerg, Denmark. It consists of an upturned wooden open fishing boat sitting on a low wooden wall and covered in tarred canvas.

These hog boats have been cut in half and stood upright for use as rope and net stores by fishermen on Brighton beach in the 1820s.

The whale catcher *Karrakatta* was built in Norway in 1912 and sent out to work for the West Australian Whaling Co. which was owned by Norwegians. At an unknown date it steamed thousands of miles to South Georgia Island to be based at Husvik whaling station. When replaced by more modern catchers, it was dragged ashore and the boiler was used to supply steam to run the machines in the workshop nearby.

This Mersey buoy vessel was placed ashore as a signpost for the Fun Ship and has been used for carrying a large political banner headed 'Corruption in Flintshire' with a website address.

CHAPTER FIVE

THE BREAKER'S YARD

The term 'shipbreaking' sounds very destructive and disreputable. The American word 'shipwrecking' is even worse and carries overtones of wanton destruction. Newspaper reports have often referred to a ship-breaker's yard as a 'graveyard of ships', yet the sole reason for breaking up ships when they come to the end of their useful time is a sound economic one and in today's terms a 'green' one as well, as breaking up ships releases the materials in their hulls, engines and equipment for further use. Metal scrap, which is the main end product of shipbreaking, can be re-melted to make new steel plates for more ships and valuable non-ferrous metals such as copper and phosphor bronze can be recycled. Much of the equipment can be salvaged and sold second-hand for use in other ships or for use ashore. A large passenger liner, so far as the passenger accommodation is concerned, is no more than a floating hotel and, while the outer hull and the engines might be worn out, the interiors – beds, chairs, pots, pans, china and much else – can all be auctioned off to all sorts of other users.

Sentiment clouds the end of a ship, particularly if it was a famous liner or a warship with battle honours. Their 'passing' has been mourned as if they were sentient beings. This can be felt, for example, in J.M.W. Turner's masterpiece 'The Fighting Temeraire', which must be one of the most reproduced paintings of all time. This painting, held in the National Gallery, depicts one of the warships that took a major role in winning the Battle of Trafalgar being towed up the Thames by a paddle tug to Rotherhithe to be broken up in 1838. The painting reflects the romantic melancholy of witnessing the passing of this gallant ship. It is also more than a documentary record of a sad event because it symbolises the passing of the Age of Sail, with the fussy steam tug taking charge of the majestic sailing battleship, and the wider radical changes that affected early nineteenth-century Britain. In more recent years there have indeed been press and fundraising campaigns to save some of this type of 'heroic' vessel. The aircraft carrier HMS *Ark Royal* of 1950 was the subject of a famous television documentary (with Rod Stewart's *Sailing* as a theme song) and this fame led to a campaign to save it from the breaker's yard. In the event it was far too big and expensive to make preservation feasible, but many relics, such as the bell

There is always a feeling of great sadness when a fine and long-serving liner leaves for the breaker's yard. This was reinforced in the case of the *Britannic* because it was the last but one of the White Star liners. Launched from Harland & Wolff's shipyard in 1930, the *Britannic* was an innovative twin-screw motor ship. It was taken over by Cunard in 1934 but continued to sail in the White Star colours. *Britannic*'s last voyage ended at Liverpool on 4 December and twelve days later it sailed from Liverpool under its own power to the breaker's yard at Inverkeithing on the Firth of Forth.

and nameplates, were saved for display in museums by the national papers. The P&O liner *Canberra* of 1960, which became famous as 'the great white whale' troopship of the 1982 Falklands War, was also the subject of another unsuccessful preservation campaign. The gradual process of breaking up fine old vessels is always a sad sight, as they are shorn of their distinctive funnels and superstructure. Yet it was, and continues to be, a necessary business. Ships were and are big capital investments and there is money to be recouped by selling them for scrap when they can no longer continue sailing. The materials of their hull, engines, equipment and internal fittings all have a value. As we will see later on, the memory of some ships has been perpetuated by the survival of parts of their structure, or fixtures and fittings – often in strange surroundings.

Shipbreaking as we understand it today seems to have started with the breaking up of high-quality wooden vessels and the reuse of their timbers in new vessels or for other purposes such as house building or furniture making. A wooden ship's hull consists of lots of individual components fastened by hundreds of fastenings – bolts, nails and spikes. Dismantling was therefore a labour-intensive process and only justified if there were worthwhile materials to be recovered. Ships which had been

Breaking up a wooden ship, especially a large one, was difficult and time consuming because of the hundreds of bolts and spikes that held the wooden frames and planking together. This East Indiaman, *Canton*, was sunk into the shore of the Thames as a small dry dock in 1829 and was finally broken up in 1898. It was so well built that it had to be smashed apart.

Left: In 1999, the Mersey flat *Ruth Bate* was broken up at Widnes, on the north bank of the upper Mersey. Built in 1953, it ceased commercial cargo carrying in the 1960s and was converted into a floating base for the Maghull branch of the St John Ambulance Service and in the 1980s was towed to Widnes for preservation. It lay there, sunk and deteriorating, without any funds for restoration. The local council considered it an eyesore and a danger and arranged to have it refloated and brought ashore.

Below: The bow of the *Ruth Bate* has had the deck planks levered off but the task of pulling apart the solid frames and planking which were fastened together with hand-forged bolts proved quite difficult in spite of the years of neglect.

Shipbreaking yards were usually sited away from the main port areas with good access to their main customers, the steel makers. This painting depicted the breaker's yard at Hale Head, ten miles inland from the port of Liverpool. There was a railway siding to carry away the scrap to steel works in Lancashire including those at Manchester, Wigan and Widnes. The two ships being broken up are two of the ferry steamers which plied to Eastham from Liverpool until the ferry closed in 1929.

built with copper fastenings and sheathed with copper sheets to protect their hulls from wooden boring creatures were sometimes burnt just to recover their copper. The breaking up of old warships certainly took place in the naval dockyards. This has been confirmed by the recent discovery of a large collection of frame timbers in the floor of the wheelwright's workshop at Chatham Dockyard. There was a large number of surplus warships after the end of the Napoleonic War in 1815 and some of these were sold to private civilian firms for breaking up. The firm of Henry Castle & Son, established on the Thames at Baltic Wharf, Mill Bank in 1838, came to specialise in old warships and was officially named as an 'Admiralty Shipbreaking Yard' in 1864. The company supplied timber to the building trade and their second yard at Long's Wharf, Woolwich had half an acre of land used for cutting up ship timbers and laying them out for sale. Many of the warships that fell into their hands were constructed from teak instead of – or as well as – the traditional English oak. Castles exploited their stocks of teak in a novel way in 1880: they began converting the recovered teak into furniture. They launched a range of 'Teakwood Garden Seats, Chairs and Tables' and it was their teak seats that graced the gardens of Buckingham Palace for Queen Victoria's Golden Jubilee celebrations in 1887. It was Sidney Castle who had thought up the idea of converting ship timbers into garden furniture. His simple and elegant designs became models for seating in public parks. He also had a flair for marketing; when the firm bought the wooden warship HMS *Southampton*, he produced a catalogue and contacted former officers and distributed it in South Africa where the ship had been based for a long time.

Shipbreaking is a messy business generally conducted on a muddy foreshore. It is not surprising that bits and pieces are left behind long after shipbreaking has ceased. These two pieces of plating with their riveted fastenings were found on the beach at New Ferry on the Mersey's south bank. This was the site of the scrapping of the *Great Eastern*. Could these be the last remnants of the huge hull of Brunel's wonder ship?

Others copied his example. In 1897, breakers of one of Nelson's ships, HMS *Foudroyant* of 1798, recovered large quantities of timber and copper which they turned into all kinds of appropriately inscribed small souvenirs for sale to the tourists visiting Blackpool. Other major ship-breakers, including T.W. Ward at Morecambe and Preston or Hughes Bolckow at Blyth, north of Newcastle, advertised their own ranges of garden furniture from the early 1900s. Hughes Bolckow had the added advantage of recruiting Sidney Castle in 1904 when Castle's family firm went bankrupt that year.

The *Lonsdale* was a 1,756-ton, three-masted, full-rigged ship built at Londonderry in 1889 for Liverpool owners. In 1909, it arrived at Stanley in the Falklands after a fire and storm damage. Condemned by the surveyors as unseaworthy and sold for use as a hulk at Punta Arenas, Chile, *Lonsdale* lies there today partly scrapped and classified as a piece of national maritime heritage.

The interior of the *Lonsdale* shows the breaker's technique of starting at the stern and working down to the waterline. It looks as if they suddenly stopped work, leaving the stern framing intact.

T.W. Ward & Co. had a major shipbreaking centre on the tidal River Ribble at Preston which was kept busy with a mixture of small warships and merchant ships. The *W.S. Patterson* was a 276-ton paddle steamer built in 1876 as a salvage vessel for the Mersey Docks and Harbour Board. In 1903, the Board had it converted into a grain barge. In 1950, it was sold to William Cooper Ltd as a sand barge and was sent for scrapping in 1966.

The *Great Eastern* was the first iron ship to attract attention when it was broken up in 1889. The ship had been the ultimate design of Isambard Brunel, that most versatile and visionary engineer. Launched in 1858, the *Great Eastern* had been a ship before its time. With a tonnage of almost 19,000 tons, it was the largest ship ever built by a wide margin. Equipped with sails, paddles and a screw propeller, it was intended to provide a steam liner service direct to Australia via the Cape of Good Hope without stopping to replenish the bunkers. In the event, technical and financial problems meant that it was never used for its original purpose. After a few unprofitable voyages to New York, it was taken out of service and converted into a telegraph cable-laying ship. The *Great Eastern* laid four ocean telegraph cables but spent much time laid up. Its final role was as a touring exhibition and funfair ship for Lewis's, a Liverpool department store. In 1888, it was sold to Henry Bath & Co. metal brokers and beached at New Ferry on the south bank of the River Mersey.

Here, members of the public are wandering around the cruiser HMS *Glasgow* at Ward's Preston yard. Many ships were opened to the public at a cost of a shilling or 6*d*. This view from 1926 was taken shortly after the Glasgow arrived and before breaking had started in earnest. HMS *Glasgow* has already been partly stripped, though, as the guns and lifeboats have been removed, most likely for reuse in another Navy vessel.

The most famous ship to be broken at Ward's in Morecambe was the White Star Line vessel RMS *Majestic*. This ship was destined for the breakers in 1912, but the sinking of the *Titanic* gave the ship two years of extra passenger life as it was drafted back into service to partner the *Olympic* on the company's Southampton-New York sailings. It arrived at Morecambe in May 1914 and was opened to the public almost as soon as it arrived. Here it's dressed in bunting on the day of arrival. Within a few months the *Majestic* had been cut up and recycled.

There was a five-day auction sale of all the fixtures and fittings which realised £38,000. Some of these relics have survived close to the site of the ship's scrapping in the Great Eastern pub at New Ferry. The *Great Eastern* was seen as an unlucky ship and popular legend explained that this was because a riveter and his boy helper had been entombed in the double bottom during its construction. This story followed the ship all the way to its breaking up and it was said (though never proved) that two skeletons were found in the bottom of the hull. The hull itself was formed from massive plates and girders all riveted together and it took many months to take them apart because there were no oxyacetylene torches in 1889. Many labourers with cold chisels and sledge hammers cut the heads off the thousands of rivets and levered the pieces of metal apart. The plates had to be cut into smaller pieces so that they could be thrown into the melting furnace and this was done by scoring the plate with a diamond cutter and chiselling out a groove along the score mark. The plate would then be turned over and hit with a sledge hammer to break it into two. Cast-iron components were smashed into small pieces by a giant steel ball which was hauled up a derrick and then dropped on them. The scrap was then loaded into barges for carriage to steel mills further up the Mersey.

The market for scrap gradually developed. In 1863, the Martin brothers of Angoûleme, France discovered a method of melting scrap metal with pig iron. The resulting mix could then be used in steel making. Other innovations in steel making helped increase production, while the decreasing cost of making steel meant that it could be used for a wider range of products. It was an attractive material for shipbuilders because it was stronger and lighter than wrought iron, and increasing numbers of ships began to be built in steel rather than wrought iron from the 1880s. The demand for scrap rose accordingly and shipbreaking became an essential adjunct to this demand. The shipbreaking industry rose from a kind of cottage industry to a big business in 1904. In that year the Royal Navy started the wholesale clearout of old and obsolete vessels that cluttered up its dockyards. The Navy was engaged in re-equipping with Dreadnought-class battleships and turbine-engined cruisers and destroyers as part of its deadly competition with its arch rival – the German Navy. Liner companies, especially on the Atlantic, were also discarding older ships and building very large vessels, such as the 45,000-ton sisters *Olympic* and *Titanic*, to beat their competitors. This also ensured a good supply of ships for breaking up. Both naval and mercantile sources of old ships dried up in the First World War because every ship, however ancient, took on a new value because of the huge number of ships sunk by German submarines. But 1919, at the end of the war, was a boom year for shipbreaking as large numbers of captured or redundant warships were released. This prompted new speculators to plunge into the market and this caused bitter complaints from the established group of eight major firms. All too soon the boom ended in a slump and even the large firms such as Hughes Bolckow struggled. The 1926 Washington Treaty brought further warships on to the market as the main naval powers agreed to limit their fleets.

The Swansea Maritime and Industrial Museum has the only display on shipbreaking that I have ever seen. It includes a portable motor winch that could be lifted on to a ship being broken up for lifting equipment and metal fragments down to ground level.

The Canadian Pacific liner RMS *Empress* of Scotland arrived at Blyth on 4 December 1930, for breaking up. Three days later it was opened to the public for inspection with the proceeds going to the local hospital. A fire started on board on Wednesday 10 December and the ship was gutted with the loss of £11,000 worth of furniture and panelling.

Left: The oxyacetylene cutting torch revolutionised the shipbreaking process. The tanker *San Sylvestre* in the foreground has been cut down at Bo'ness on the Firth of Forth and, in the background, the liner *Columbia* has been stripped of its fittings and awaits the cutter's torch.

Below: The French passenger liner *L'Atlantique* has been partially dismantled at Port Glasgow on the Clyde in 1935. The breakers have started at the stern and reduced this down to the bilges. The third funnel has just been taken down. Ultimately the hull will be reduced down to its double bottom which can be dragged ashore for the final act of destruction.

The deck of the 22,500-ton battleship HMS *Orion* (being broken up at Queenborough on the Medway in 1922) shows the scale of operation needed to break up a major naval vessel. The guns and their turrets have been removed and two cranes on a railway track have been installed on the main deck to assist with the lift of the severed sections of steel ashore. Warships were more complicated to dismantle because of their thick belts of amour plating and their many compartments.

The 1930s saw the disposal of famous liners such as the Cunard Line's *Mauretania* of 1907. Its scrapping at Rosyth in 1934 caused much press interest. *Mauretania*'s final passage up the Firth of Forth was recorded in a large oil painting by Charles Pears, a leading marine artist. This work was hung in one of the public areas of its successor, the *Queen Mary* of 1936. With the outbreak of the Second World War in September 1939, shipbreaking again came to a standstill as every vessel was needed. The Shaw Savill liner *Tainui* had arrived at Blyth ready to be broken up when it was officially requisitioned and put back into service.

Ship-breakers took part in the campaign to salvage all possible useful materials by salvaging wrecked ships. Scrapping resumed in earnest immediately after the war but under tight official control. There were also to be mergers among the main players. By the 1960s, shipbuilding, steel making and shipbreaking was starting to move away from the traditional centres in Britain to the Indian sub-continent and this trend continued into the twenty-first century.

TEAK
GARDEN FURNITURE
Made from Timbers of Dismantled Battleships.

THE 'ALBION' GARDEN SET
3ft. x 3ft. x 2ft. 4ins. high,

£14 14s. per Set.

The "Edgar" Seat
1ft. 6ins. x 3ft. 2ins. high x 1ft. 10ins. wide.

The "Rodney" Table
2ft. 7ins. x 2ft. x 2ft. 6ins. high.

£4 15s. each   £3 3s. each.

TEAK FOOTBOARDS.

Sizes to Match Seats, 2/6 per foot run. Made to any size or design

SHRUB BOX	TEAK GARDEN GATES
2ft. 6ins. x 1ft. 5ins.	Made to any size and design.
£2 10s.	Speciality : STEERING WHEEL CENTRE GATES.

Prices F.O.R. Morecambe.
5% Discount Cash with Order.

Teak from wooden warships or the deck planking of steamers could be converted into highly saleable garden furniture. This was an advertisement for articles made from the teak planking of naval vessels broken up by T.W. Ward & Co. at Morecambe.

Shipbreaking was a hard, yet profitable undertaking. The ship-breaker had to learn his trade on the job; there were no text books or training courses. The ability to improvise and be ingenious was essential. Every ship presented different problems: a ship-breaker had to know both how a ship was put together and also to have confidence in the abilities of his workforce to take one apart. Henry Castle & Son, who had specialised in wooden warships, realised that they had taken on too much when they bought the iron battleship HMS *Ajax* in 1904. They found that they did not have the expertise to dismantle the armour plating and, as a result, they lost money because it took far too long to break the ship up, eventually having to put their business into the hands of the receiver. Most of the ships were sold by auction or by public tender and ship-breakers were in competition with each other and with foreign buyers. Some ships had come straight out of service and had lots of working equipment on board that could be sold at a good price; others were rust buckets which had been laid up for years with little or poor material in them. Naval vessels had lots of brass and other non-ferrous fittings but their armour plating and their division into lots of small compartments meant they took more time to break up.

1 This replica of the *Golden Hind* gives an excellent impression of the main features of a late sixteenth-century ship, including the versatile, three-masted rig and gunports for firing the ship's armament.

2 Tugs were among the first viable steamships and they improved the safety and turnround of sailing ships by being able to tow them in and out of port whatever the state of the wind. Paddles made them highly manoeuvrable and many remained in service well into the twentieth century.

3 The Dover Boat, which dates from the Bronze Age, was discovered in 1992. It was probably about 40 foot long and flat bottomed, with its planks fastened together by an elaborate system of cleats carved out of the planks, battens and stitching with yew withies. It would have been capable of being paddled across the Channel with up to 3 tons of cargo.

6583   H. M. S. "Resolution"   (14150 tons 2nd Cl. Battleship).

CUNARD R.M.S. "LUSITANIA & MAURETANIA"

4 *Opposite above:* Screw-propelled steamers with compound engines and high-pressure boilers offered sufficient economy to compete with sailing ships in many valuable trades. The *Cognac* of 1860 was typical of many because it still carried sails as a means of fuel economy and also as a way of making port if the engines broke down.

5 *Opposite below:* By 1892, the date of the launching of the battleship HMS *Resolution*, the Royal Navy had finally abandoned sails and the main armament of heavy-calibre, breach-loading guns was installed in revolving turrets. The tall masts were retained for signalling and after 1900 also carried the first wireless aerials.

6 *Left:* Steam turbines were another important technical breakthrough which enabled 'super liners' such as Cunard's *Lusitania* to sustain speeds in excess of 26 knots.

7 *Below:* The launch (or birth) of a ship was always an occasion for celebration. Everards, the coaster owners, issued a special postcard of the painting of the launch of their 100th vessel – the *Centurity* – at Goole in 1956.

LAUNCH OF OUR 100TH VESSEL, M.V. "CENTURITY" AT GOOLE, YORKSHIRE

10 *Above:* Broken where it went ashore, this was one of the light floats – miniature unmanned lightships – which marked the port side of the main approach channel into the port of Liverpool.

11 *Left:* Lightships are strongly built with plenty of accommodation and have been converted to all kinds of stationary uses, including restaurants, and in this case for use by the Colchester Sea Cadet unit.

8 *Opposite above:* The *Louise* of 1869 was once a proud American 'Downeaster' that was reduced to a coal hulk at Grytviken, South Georgia Island in 1904 before being beached. Its rotting hull was set alight in the 1980s and very little remains above the waterline.

9 *Opposite below:* The *Brutus* started carrying cargoes as the *Sierra Pedrosa* for Thompson Anderson & Co. in 1883. Their ships were noted for their well-kept appearance with their white-painted hulls. It became the coal hulk *Brutus* at Prince Olav whaling station, South Georgia Island in 1911 and today is a sunken, rusting wreck.

12 *Above:* When the Cunard Line found that the demand for regular transatlantic passenger services had declined because of competition from jet air liners, they transferred their modern liners to cruising. The *Saxonia* of 1954 was refitted as the cruise liner *Carmania* in 1963.

13 *Below:* Scottish shipbuilding yards have produced many fine, wooden, motor fishing vessels (MFVs). Their fine construction and sea-keeping qualities have made them common subjects for conversion into pleasure cruisers, such as this example docked at Ipswich in 2002.

14 *Top:* Smaller types of traditional ships such as Thames barges can be kept sailing and earn a living providing sailing holidays or corporate hospitality. The *Pudge* of 1920 is one of two barges run by the Thames Barge Sailing Club.

15 *Above:* This is a more unusual conversion of a military vessel. This Second World War amphibious DUKW (the code letters for this type of vehicle) has been converted to provide land and water tours in Liverpool under the name of the *Wacker Quacker*

16 *Left:* The Admiralty used the Scottish design for a class of MFVs during the Second World War and when they have been sold out of the service they have found new uses, such as this cruising restaurant based at Orford on the River Alde.

17 The tug *Brocklebank* of 1964 is owned by Merseyside Maritime Museum and kept running by a dedicated team of volunteers. It flies the flag for the museum at maritime festivals all around the country.

18 It is difficult to run and maintain larger vessels afloat. This is why it was decided that the 700-ton Liverpool pilot cutter *Edmund Gardner* had to be permanently dry-docked. Visitors can go on board and all the interior has been fitted out as if it was still a working ship, even down to the noise and vibration of the diesels.

19 Even fragments of ships can be valuable historical relics. This piece of ironwork is a sample of the patent iron fastenings on the Liverpool ship *Jhelum*. This fragment was carried by the brigantine *Soren Larsen* from the Falkland Islands to Liverpool in 1992.

The ship-breaker needed a shrewd appreciation of what he might make from his purchase and how long it would take to break it up before he sent in his bid. He also needed to know his market for scrap and have a ready source of money so that he could seize opportunities as they arose. It could not be described as 'a steady trade'. Capital was also needed to invest in facilities and these became more complex as the size of ships increased. In 1904, for example, Thomas Ward turned his business into a limited company and issued £350,000 of shares to finance the expansion of his business. Some of the major firms had direct links to the big steel makers. Richard Hughes was a metal merchant who built up a flourishing scrap business on the Tyne. In 1908 he went into partnership with Charles Bolckow, the son of a Middlesbrough steel maker who had married the daughter of Sir Arthur Dorman, the head of the biggest firm of steel makers in the North East. Bolckow was not directly employed in steel making but had experience in selling scrap and engineering equipment. Their new company was able to sell some of its shares to Sir Arthur Dorman and thus create a valuable link to one of their main customers. There were to be occasions in the later life of the company when Dormans stood guarantor for them when the banks were threatening them with foreclosure. Thomas Ward, the other leading ship-breaker, started a coal and coke business in 1878, specialising in supplying companies operating foundries and blast furnaces. In 1881 he spotted an opportunity to expand into selling his customers scrap metal as well. This in turn led to the establishment of his Ship Dismantling Department in 1894. This new venture meant acquiring a site at Preston on the tidal River Ribble, which was to be in continuous use until the 1960s, and a temporary berth at Barrow-in-Furness where there was surplus quay space in the docks and a major steel works close at hand.

Once the ship-breaker had his funding, there was then a whole series of detailed requirements needed in order to be successful in business. He needed an accessible quay with an adjacent tidal dock or basin. It also had to be cheap to rent; he could not compete for space in the major ports. At the same time they also needed good rail, road or water access to transport the scrap to their customers. Shipbreaking yards tended to be on the margins of major steel-making regions: the Firth of Forth, North East and Yorkshire, Lancashire and South Wales. If he intended to demolish the largest class of ships such as battleships and liners, he would need a good depth of water at high tide, at least 30 to 35 feet. This was one of the early problems for Hughes Bolckow. Their first yard was sited on the upper section of the River Tyne, above Newcastle at Derwenthaugh. In 1909, they bought their first large warship, the 9,150-ton HMS *Collingwood* built in 1889. Its dismantling had to start downstream at Dunston on moorings and using a floating crane. It took a year to reduce its draught sufficiently to be towed up the river. Their next warship, HMS *Barfleur*, got stuck near the Tyne swing bridge and caused chaos in Newcastle and Gateshead. It was not surprising that the firm moved its main operation to Blyth, a coal port with spare space to the north of the busy Tyne. Nevertheless, there were still problems with getting the bigger vessels into the harbour and the harbour authorities were rightly worried that a large vessel might block the harbour entrance. In the end the firm had to spend large amounts of money dredging a deeper berth

The clutter in the foreground is the remains of the Liverpool Landing Stage which was built in 1876 and lasted for a century. The two vessels were the Mersey Docks and Harbour Board's two steam buoy maintenance and salvage vessels the *Vigilant* and the *Salvor*, which were replaced by a single, modern, diesel-powered *Vigilant* in 1978.

alongside their quay. The process of 'unbuttoning' a ship was a matter of hand work which needed hard manual labour. It was not particularly well paid and it was dangerous. A pool of readily available workmen was a further essential. In the slump of the early 1930s, part of the government's schemes to create work in the worst areas of unemployment was to use shipbreaking. The Cunard liner *Berengaria*, for example, was towed to Jarrow on the Tyne for breaking up to make jobs for some of the many men who were out of work in the area. While the introduction of oxyacetylene cutting during the First World War speeded up the dismantling process, it also added to the cost of dismantling. Wards at Morecambe first used it only for the thicker plates because of the expense. The cost of transporting large numbers of portable oxygen cylinders became so high that by 1923 they installed their own oxygen-making plant and generated their own acetylene from calcium carbide and seawater. The old hammer and chisel workers were still used, though in decreasing numbers. One of their jobs was to chip through the accumulated paint to speed up the cutting. This could be as much as an inch thick and was known at the Morecambe yard as 'crab fat'. Gas cutting also carried the added risk of setting fire to the vessel, as the tanks and the engine rooms often contained residues of oil and grease. Hughes Bolckow kept two portable fire engines at their Blyth yard.

In 1930 they bought the Canadian Pacific liner *Empress of Scotland*. This was a good purchase because it had just been refitted and had magnificent furnishings. Early on 10 December, the watchmen discovered a fire on board. It had already taken hold and the efforts of the local fire brigade, the harbour fire float and the employees were all in vain and it had to be scuttled to put out the fire. £11,000 was lost in furnishings, timber and equipment. One of the first tasks after a ship arrived was to strip out all furnishings including wooden panelling and deck planks. Then the superstructure would be taken down and this lightened the vessel. A further series of cutting operations took the ship's hull down deck by deck until all that was left was the double bottom that could be winched on to the shore for the final dismantling.

On the shore side, there had to be cranes to lift the dismantled pieces ashore. At Morecambe, Wards had several rail-mounted 5- and 10-ton steam cranes and a massive sheerlegs with a 90-ton capacity for lifting out boilers and pieces of machinery. The breaking ball for breaking up cast iron was also located ashore and electrically powered sheers capable of slicing up larger pieces were another important piece of equipment in the more modern yards. There also had to be space for storing different metals and covered storage for furniture and fittings. There might also be a woodwork shop for converting ship timbers into furniture and a showroom which could be used for auctions. Security was also important with so many valuable metals and portable items. The breaking up beach at New Ferry was often raided at night by the local bargemen who rowed ashore with muffled oars to see what they could loot from the ships awaiting breaking up. Good transport was another important requirement. This meant a direct rail link to a main line railway, with sidings to store wagons and possibly a locomotive.

There was also a need to be a 'good neighbour'. Shipbreaking created noise and dirt and was generally unsightly. It was not so bad if the yard was at a distance from housing and amenities, but at Morecambe in 1904, for example, Ward's yard was sited in the old cross-Channel ferry terminal and this bordered the seaside promenade. While the local town council welcomed Ward's contribution to the local economy, they disliked the noise and the mess. Ward's started a public relations campaign to counter the criticisms. They opened up their latest acquisition – HMS *Raleigh* – to visitors and the admissions income at threepence per head was donated to the local cottage hospital. They continued this policy of opening up new arrivals to visitors, but in the end the council and the London, Midland & Scottish Railway Co. who owned the yard forced Ward's to cease shipbreaking in 1932. It simply did not fit in with trying to promote a seaside resort. The site was cleared of all its unsightly piles of scrap iron and in its place the railway company built a smart art deco hotel to attract new visitors. Shipbreaking today raises the same concerns together with added worries over the pollution of the local environment with oil, poisonous chemicals or asbestos and concern for the health and safety of the labour force. In the past, lead poisoning from burning lead-based paint and lack of safety clothing were treated as a fact of life. Today most shipbreaking is carried out abroad, with India and Bangladesh as market leaders. Organisations that campaign for improving the environment, such as Greenpeace, have the improvement of the ship-breaker's yards on their agenda.

Above: Breaking up large ships has moved away from British shores to India and the Far East. Smaller ships which would not be profitable if sent long distance for dismantling are still broken up in the UK. The Leander class anti-submarine frigate HMS *Euryalus*, built in 1965, was about to be torched in 1994 at Millom on the remote Duddon estuary at a former iron ore exporting quay.

Opposite: The breaking up of the *Chirripo* (II) on 5 September 1952 at Preston shows just how destructive the demolishing of a ship can be. It's been cut down almost to the main deck and the effects of the breaker's torch can clearly be seen. The main mast has gone, leaving only a stump, as have the funnel and hatch covers, and the anchors and chains. Soon it will no longer exist as a ship, but only as a memory for those who sailed on it. This view was taken just under six months after the *Chirripo* (II)'s arrival at the yard.

Shipbreaking in the United Kingdom continues in a small way today. There are no more giant battleships to dismantle and large merchant ships are invariably sent to the East. Smaller ships such as coasters, fishing boats, ferries and naval vessels are not worth being sailed thousands of miles to be broken up. The 'glory days' of British shipbreaking have long gone, never to return. But some of the ships' salvaged materials have survived; furnishing and panelling which was often of high quality can be seen in pubs and hotels, while brass artefacts such as bells have been preserved in large numbers, and we shall be looking at some specific examples in chapter nine.

The motor barge *Sealand Trader* was waiting for cutting up at Queenborough where shipbreaking was still continued in 2001. The vessel moored behind it is a cut-down motor coaster which has been converted into a workshop and crane barge.

POST CARD

CARTE POSTALE.

POSTKARTE

S.S. Minnekahda (Triple Screw) runs between London and New York. Gross tonnage 17,281 tons, h.p. 11,250, length 646 ft., breadth 66 ft., depth 52 ft. She is unique in being the only Atlantic liner carrying tourist third cabin passengers only.

(FOR ADDRESS ONLY.)

This ship is now being broken up at Dalmuir and we have for sale Furnishings and Fittings from the accommodation for 1,000 passengers.

Also Auxiliary Plant, Boats and Good Timber.

OUR 'PHONE No. IS CHANGED TO :

Clydebank 570   Private Exchange.

ARNOTT, YOUNG & CO.
(Shipbreakers), Ltd.

Messrs. Barnes & Bell, Ltd.,

79, St. George's Place,

GLASGOW, C. 2.

The reverse of a postcard of the Atlantic Transport liner SS *Minnekahda* advertising the sale of its furnishings and fittings. Most likely the postcard was one of many found on board when the ship was sold for scrapping and has been recycled itself to advertise the sale of the contents.

CHAPTER SIX

SHIPWRECKS AND MARITIME ACCIDENTS

In the days when ships were solely dependent on the wind for their propulsion, there were numerous shipwrecks and thousands of sailors drowned. In the nineteenth century, around the British Isles alone hundreds of ships might be wrecked in one night's winter gale. For example, the *Norfolk Annals* recorded that on 11 February 1807 the brig HMS *Snipe* was lost just south of Great Yarmouth with the loss of sixty lives, including some French prisoners of war, and another twelve merchant ships were cast ashore between Great Yarmouth and Cromer. Gore's *Liverpool Annals* recorded 'a terrific and most destructive hurricane' on 6 January 1839 when two New York packets and an emigrant ship were all blown ashore at the entrance to the River Mersey with the loss of over a hundred lives. Gore later recorded the loss of one of the biggest ships of the time, the 2,756-ton *Royal Charter*, with over 400 passengers and crew drowned on 26 October 1859. The *Royal Charter* was only one of 343 ships wrecked in that gale. These are just random examples and the Board of Trade's statistics collected from 1850 onwards showed there was a growing number of wrecks. Between 1850 and 1854 it stood at an annual average 969, but between 1859 and 1864 it had risen to 1,664. This was partly because the Mercantile Marine was expanding rapidly. The government was pressurised to intervene to provide greater regulation for shipping industry for its own good. This included provision of compulsory certificates of competence for officers and masters and compulsory load lines to ensure ships were not overloaded.

Many of the disasters that occurred left their remains behind on the seabed and this chapter concentrates on them. There are also important maritime survivors on dry land or on the foreshore, and these are covered in the next chapter. Underwater remains can provide valuable insights into the past development of ships. For much of the past there is no written record and we are dependent on archaeological discoveries for extending our knowledge. Where a wreck has lain uncontaminated, it can prove to be a real 'time capsule'. Such wreck sites can also yield large numbers of artefacts which can tell us about what people used and valued, and also what

Opposite above: This was a common sight in the days of sail: a coasting schooner grounded ashore either through pressure of weather or human error. At the time this picture was taken there was still some prospect of savaging the vessel, but a fresh gale would have strained or even broken up its hull.

Opposite below: Ships could be sunk through carrying too much cargo. This eighteenth-century slate barge was sunk in Llyn Peris with a cargo of slate and was rediscovered by divers 200 years later, salvaged, conserved and displayed at Electric Mountain, Llanberis.

Right: The master of the *William Turner* lost his bearings on his final approach to Liverpool at the end of his long voyage and went ashore and broke up. The figurehead was saved as a souvenir by the Wynn family of Belan Fort, close to the site of the wreck.

trading connections they maintained. Even in distant times sea trade could be conducted over long distances. For example divers have found a large quantity of foreign bronze axes and spears which (because of their broken condition) appear to have been en route for Britain from France in the Bronze Age for melting down. The axes were of a different design to the local ones and could have only come from the mainland. The vessel that carried them has disappeared but this cache is a witness to an unsuspected trade. Thus shipwrecks and their cargoes can rewrite the existing accounts of pre-history. In this case, the find has changed popular thinking about the distribution of a particular type of axe and demonstrated that there was more cross-Channel trade than suspected.

Sale of Wreck, Strona

A common sight after the loss of a ship was the sale of the wreck. The items salvaged – including lifeboats, cargo, wood and anything else recovered – were sold. This rare postcard view from Strona, Caithness shows the sale of wreck from a stranded sailing vessel some time in the late 1890s or early 1900s.

Some of this material can be immensely valuable, such as the gold and jewellery from sunken Spanish ships in the West Indies or cargoes of Chinese porcelain found in south-east Asian waters. Such treasures are a constant temptation for salvage projects, which are mainly concerned with recovery and not the careful recording of the position of objects and the remains of the wreck. A systematic plan of a wreck and its contents is an essential part of the archaeological method because it ensures that all possible information has been recovered. Archaeological excavation and salvage are both destructive and usually damage a shipwreck site for all time. Today it is possible to discover more and more wrecks even in the very deepest parts of the ocean, and both archaeologists and salvors have access to a wide range of devices to identify and excavate these sunken ships.

There are many causes of marine accidents. We have already seen that the force of the weather can play a large part. If a vessel loses its watertight integrity the sea can get into the hull and make it unstable and liable to capsize. This can occur when hatches or watertight doors have been left open or smashed. In 1987 the cross-Channel ferry the *Herald of Free Enterprise* capsized outside Zeebrugge Harbour because its bow doors had not been closed. Mersey flats, which were a type of local sailing barge, quite often sailed empty without their hatch covers and

Central ladder or bucket dredgers, with their central chain of buckets driven from a high machinery superstructure, could be vulnerable to capsizing. The dredger *Walter H. Glynn* capsized in the Mersey while working off Gladstone Dock entrance in the 1920s. It looked as if this was its final resting place, but the experienced and well-equipped Mersey Docks and Harbour Board salvage team succeeded in rescuing it.

tarpaulins battened down to save time. Their two hatches took up most of the length of their hulls and a sudden squall could easily overwhelm them. This happened to the flat *Samson*, which was lost in December 1898 after its skipper was hastening to catch the tide. He had failed to cover the hatches and, as he left the shelter of Garston Dock, a squall caught his barge broadside and capsized her. Deep-sea sailing ships could be caught in a similar way and be rolled over and sunk without trace. Two of the most famous shipwrecks, Henry VIII's warship *Mary Rose* and Gustavus Adolphus of Sweden's new flagship, the *Vasa*, were both overwhelmed when caught broadside with their lower gunports open. Overloaded vessels were also at risk even on inland waters. The late eighteenth-century boat raised from the bottom of Llyn Padarn lake in North Wales was found to be carrying too many slates and must have been overwhelmed by a sudden squall coming down from the surrounding mountains.

Cargo shifting in the hold was another common cause of loss in heavy weather. Grain, for example, had to be carefully loaded with adequate shifting boards to prevent it from moving in the hold, as a shifting grain cargo could capsize the ship. If grain was allowed to drop into the bilges it could also choke the ship's pumps. Coal, another very common cargo, also had to be treated with respect.

Above: Fire was a terrible hazard for ships, especially wooden ones. The famous emigrant clipper, the *Lightning* of 1854, was set ablaze by spontaneous combustion of its cargo of wool bales and had to be left to burn to the waterline and sink at Geelong, Australia in 1869.

Below: Steam ships can be set ablaze and abandoned. The Danish cargo ship *Marie Maersk* caught fire in Caernarfon Bay while on passage from Shanghai to Liverpool on 22 March 1927. The crew were rescued and the *Marie Maersk* was allowed to drift ashore near Holyhead. This aerial picture shows that the fire had started in No.2 hold and had spread to the bridge and engine room.

It was usually loaded by tipping railway trucks into the hold and it was essential that the cargo was 'trimmed' to ensure an even distribution in the hold. Untrimmed coal cargoes could shift and at worst cause the ship to capsize. Heavy cargoes, such as copper ore or refined copper bars, could strain the structure of the hull and cause the ship to labour in heavy weather. Wool or cotton bales or other lighter cargoes, such as tea chests, were too light and needed ballast or heavy cargo placed in the bottom of the ship's hold. Guano (seabird droppings used as a powerful fertiliser), if wetted, could form a hard outer crust and shift as one body around the hold like a block of ice, causing the ship to become unstable.

Timber could also be a problematic cargo. This was partly because it was often carried in older ships which were too leaky to carry anything else and partly because extra cargo was lashed on deck. The latter was prone to shift and make the ship unstable, while it also hampered the operation of the ship.

Fire on board was another hazard that could lead to the loss of a ship. Wooden sailing ships were vulnerable. Their tarred hulls, canvas sails and hemp rigging were all readily inflammable and once a fire took hold it could consume the main timbers of the hull and burn it down to the waterline. Passenger ships were at risk because there were large numbers of often ill-disciplined people on board who had to use oil or candle lanterns in their cabins below decks. Most firms enforced strict rules about extinguishing lanterns at night and banned smoking below decks. The emigrant ship *Ocean Monarch* of the American White Diamond Line left Liverpool on 24 August 1848 with 322 steerage, thirty-two cabin passengers and forty-two crew. Having dropped its tug and set sail in a fresh breeze, fire was discovered in one of the cabins and could not be put out. It was thought to have originated from a pipe-smoking passenger. The smoke and flames created panic and 178 lives were lost. Several boats in the vicinity were able to take off the survivors, but among those lost were many who had never been to sea and became paralysed with fear. The ship was left to burn and sank some twenty miles off the coast. The charred hull, with much of its cargo of pottery intact, was rediscovered in the 1980s.

Ships also caught fire in port and many port authorities insisted there was no cooking on board while the ship was in dock to lessen the risk. One ship on fire could easily spread the danger to its neighbours. Cargoes could be inflammable; tightly packed wool, cotton bales and certain types of coal can suffer from overheating which results in spontaneous combustion, and of course special precautions are needed on vessels carrying inflammable liquids such as oil and its refined products. On 31 October 1869, the clipper ship *Lightning* was loading bales of wool at the Australian port of Geelong when fire was discovered in the fore hold. The flames spread rapidly and there was every chance they would engulf the wharf. The crew tired to drag it away using one of the capstans but the smoke and heat was too great. The mooring ropes were cut and it was allowed to drift away and sank the same day. It was rediscovered during dredging in 1931 and has since been explored by local amateur divers who recovered some of its copper sheathing and fittings.

The actual act of collision has rarely been caught on camera. Here the Elders & Fyffes steamer *Greenbrier* has been caught at the moment of hitting the Formby lightship *Star* in 1921. The *Greenbrier* escaped relatively undamaged as it struck the *Star* almost head-on.

Ships have been lost not only through their own weaknesses but also from external factors. Ships faced greater risks as they approached the coast. There were a multitude of hazards, such as submerged reefs and isolated rocks. In some parts of the ocean, especially in the North Atlantic and the approaches to Cape Horn, drifting icebergs could be as dangerous as running ashore. The most famous wreck of all time is that of the White Star liner *Titanic*, which hit an iceberg in the Atlantic in 1912.

Derelict ships abandoned by their crews, or containers lost overboard, have also been the causes of damage and sinking to unwary ships. Ships also collide with other ships, especially in restricted and busy waters close to the land. Today, the English Channel at its narrowest is divided into separate north- and south-bound routes to try and prevent collisions, but this is complicated by the many ferries plying between English ports and the Continent. Such comings together can cause repairable damage or can result in sinking, and it did not just occur with unwieldy sailing ships. Modern vessels equipped with radar and every possible navigational device can and do collide. Automatic steering systems can go wrong; often there is only a single watch keeper on the bridge and he can lose alertness through long hours or by sheer confusion from the amount of information he is confronted with. In these days, when many vessels ply under a flag of convenience, the competence of crews can vary considerably.

In the poor visibility of a storm or fog, a ship's master could lose all the usual visual clues as to his position. These included not only land or sea marks, but also being able to see the sun in order to measure its altitude in the sky and establish a ship's latitude. In 1845, the barque *William Turner* was probably no more than two days away from Liverpool with a cargo of guano loaded at Ichaboe, Peru. After covering some 7,000 miles from South America, the *William Turner* was sighted off the Smalls lighthouse on the Pembrokeshire coast. A strong gale was blowing from the south-west and the ship's master lost track of his position and failed to weather Anglesey. The barque drove ashore in Caernarfon Bay with the loss of everyone on board. All that survives is the figurehead, saved as a trophy from the shattered remains. Charles II's first yacht, the *Mary* (built in Holland in 1660) went ashore on the Skerries rocks off Anglesey in calm but foggy weather in 1675. The ballast shifted and it heeled over and sank. The remains were only rediscovered in 1971. The British Isles has many other rocky promontories and outlying rocks to trap ships and they are particularly dangerous where they lie in the track of large numbers of ships. This is what makes the reefs around the Isles of Scilly and the Lizard so dangerous, for they are in the track of the many ships coming from the Atlantic into the English Channel.

The *Star* took the full force of the impact amidships and sank, losing its light mast in the process. The Mersey Docks and Harbour Board's salvage crew raised it and it was repaired at Canning graving dock No.1 for further service. The gash caused by the collision was so large that it needed a temporary patch which has been removed to reveal the damaged area.

Offshore sandbanks in shallow waters can be as dangerous as rocks in the right conditions. At the same time they can offer protected anchorages in which ships can shelter. The Scroby Sands off Great Yarmouth formed Yarmouth Roads in which hundreds of storm- or wind-bound ships might anchor. The Downs anchorage lies between the North and South Foreland. The Goodwin Sands, which lie about six miles off the Kent coast, provide shelter from all easterly winds and the land shelter from the westerlies. It was a particularly busy anchorage during the days of sail as it was here that incoming ships picked up a pilot for the Thames and outgoing ones dropped theirs. It was also an assembly area for convoys and naval operations. The Goodwins, while offering shelter, were also a danger because of their shifting nature and many ships have either hit them by mistake or have been cast on them when their anchors or cables failed to hold them in the safety of the Downs. Ships were literally swallowed in the shifting sands only to be exposed many years later. In the Great Gale of 27 November 1703, the Royal Navy lost a squadron of four ships to the Goodwins – the *Mary*, *Stirling Castle*, *Northumberland* and *Restoration*. Extensive fieldwork by local divers has revealed the survival of all but the *Mary*. In 1979 they found the *Stirling Castle* was substantially intact, with the remains of the hull standing 29 feet clear of the seabed and with the guns and stores undamaged. But sadly by the following year this spectacular survival had been swallowed again.

For mankind, war has been a constant activity and sea warfare has become increasingly destructive as technology has advanced. In the Middle Ages, naval battles involved a variation of besieging castles on land and large bodies of soldiers boarding and fighting to capture an enemy vessel. The invention of gunpowder and cannon made it possible to also fight the enemy at a distance and sink him. The range and accuracy of weapons has continued to increase. The Dreadnought-class battleships of the early twentieth century, with their 16-inch guns, could hurl explosive shells up to twenty miles. Today, smaller-calibre guns can match that and fire faster, while guided missiles or torpedoes can be launched from surface ships, submarines or from aircraft on to targets unseen by the human eye. There were also passive weapons, especially mines, which could be exploded by contact, by sound pressure or by magnetism. The *Britannic*, the sister ship of the *Titanic*, was serving as a hospital ship in the First World War Dardanelles campaign in 1916 when it was sunk by either a mine or a torpedo. The capsized hull with its shattered bow was thoroughly explored in 1995 by Robert Ballard, the man who had found the wreck of its sister in 1986. Unfortunately there was still no conclusive evidence of what caused it to sink. Most informed opinion favours a mine, even though survivors thought they had seen the track of a torpedo speeding towards the ship. Sea battles have left a legacy of wrecks. Nelson's attack on the French fleet in the Battle of the Nile in 1798 resulted in the sinking of all but two of the French ships. Recent diving work in Aboukir Bay on the site of the battle has found many relics from these unfortunate ships. In 1918, the old British cruiser HMS *Vindictive* and other ancient warships were used as block ships to try and stop German submarines from using the port. The attack was only partially successful. When the *Vindictive* was removed after the war its bow was salvaged and mounted ashore as a permanent memorial to all those who were killed

Top: The development of powerful explosives and the deployment of mines in naval warfare has posed a new threat to ships. The steam trawler *Arctic Prince* hit a mine in the White Sea in 1916 and was lucky enough to survive the massive amount of damage to its bow.

Above: The self-propelled torpedo launched from fast surface warships and more insidiously from submarines was an even more potent weapon. In both world wars submarine attacks sank so many cargo ships that they threatened Britain's ability to continue the war. The new White Star liner *Justicia* was sunk by a torpedo on 19 July 1918. The stripes (dazzle paint) were a form of camouflage to break up the silhouette of the ship.

Above: HMS *Vindictive* was an obsolete British cruiser that was part of the raid on the Belgian port of Zeebrugge in 1918 to deny its use to German submarines.

Opposite above: Wrecked ships may break up, especially if they founder on a rocky coast, but large numbers of artefacts can survive often sealed in the ballast they carried. Charles II's yacht, *Mary*, ran into the Skerries rocks off Anglesey in 1676. The ballast mound was discovered in 1971 and a variety of objects were found in the consolidated ballast. They included silverware, cannon shot and the wooden butts of pistols (not their steel barrels which had rusted away). Items from later wrecks include the large wooden deadeye (rigging block) from a nineteenth-century ship.

Opposite below: Apart from ceramics, most objects left on underwater wrecks will deteriorate over time. If submerged in a blanket of anaerobic mud, the process can be slowed down. The auxiliary steamer *Royal Charter* was swept ashore at Moelfre, Anglesey in 1859. A series of expeditions recovered a large number of personal possessions from the passengers and crew. These included a brace of pistols which were in far better condition than those found on the *Mary*.

in this daring escapade. In 1919, at the end of the First World War, the German Navy sailed its fleet to surrender at the anchorage of Scapa Flow in the Shetland Islands. They were not well supervised and their crews robbed the victors of their prize by scuttling their ships. Most of them were subsequently raised and towed away to the breakers. The few that remain have become an underwater heritage site which divers can visit.

What happens to a ship after it has been wrecked can vary considerably. Some vessels have been cast ashore and can be salvaged for further service. Others are too damaged and have broken up where they lie. Some are wrecked on a rocky shore and are smashed to pieces. What may remain on the site are the heavy non-organic materials such as the ballast stones and the guns. The former may form a mound on the seabed and within this ballast mound smaller organic items such as small pieces of wood and leather may be preserved. This mixture of fragments may become fused together in a conglomerate of calcium carbonate, magnesium hydroxide, metal corrosion products, sand, clay, and various types of marine life such as corals, shells, barnacles and seaweeds.

Ships lost on a sandy or muddy seabed undergo change. It is likely that their upper structure will either be swept away or gradually reduced by the action of the tides, oxidation and marine creatures. In a wooden vessel, this leaves the main backbone structure of keel, keelson and the lower parts of the stempost, sternpost, frames and bottom planking. In some cases the parts of the upper structure and masts or spars can collapse into the lower portion of the hull, or the hull may have landed on the bottom on its side, leaving one side of the vessel buried and the other exposed to erosion and decay. Half the hull of the *Mary Rose* has survived in this way. The mud in which it was buried had the property of excluding most of the oxygen from the wooden hull and the wooden and other organic artefacts on board. This meant that they did not decay at the rapid rate that they would otherwise have done, had they been exposed. But the seabed is a dynamic environment and what may have been buried for centuries can be rapidly exposed. Both organic and metal objects which have been taken from such an environment need to be treated carefully. Wood, if dried out quickly, will crack and crumble. Metals will oxidise. So, in addition to the dangers and expense of pursuing archaeology underwater, there is the problem of conserving the artefacts that have been recovered. In the case of small objects that have been underwater for a short time, this may not amount to much, but if it involves the recovery of a substantial portion (or even the whole) of the hull, then the cost will run into millions of pounds and the process will take years to complete. Submerged wood, for example, may need to be strengthened by PEG (polyethylene glycol) wax, and bronze objects such as cannon may need to be subjected to many hours of electrolysis to extract the salts they have absorbed. Conservation techniques have advanced, but still remain labour intensive and expensive.

Finding wrecks underwater is by no means easy. Sometimes it is chance; the ballast mound of the Royal Yacht *Mary* was found in an obscure gully because an amateur diver happened to spot one of its bronze cannon partly exposed. There may be clues as to the position of a wreck from documents. If the ship had a valuable cargo and there was a dispute about its salvage, this could end up in the High Court of Admiralty whose archives go back to the Middle Ages. The loss of a naval vessel was the subject of a Court Martial, which would keep a detailed record of the circumstances of the loss. From the mid-eighteenth century newspapers, including the specialised maritime paper *Lloyd's List*, reported wrecks and from Victorian times the Board of Trade conducted Courts of Enquiry for major merchant shipping disasters. There are also more specific documents such as diaries of local people or local folk memories of the location of a particular wreck which have been handed down by word of mouth.

While archives may help with locating the general position of a wreck, its specific location requires a search of the seabed. Remote sensing equipment such as side scan sonar and magnetometers make the task easier. The former instruments send out a signal to map the bottom, which highlights any anomalies which could indicate a wreck. The latter measures changes in magnetic resistivity and is thus able to identify iron guns or cannonballs used as ballast. Even so, it is still possible to search many miles of seabed without getting a result. Captain John Paul Jones, the American naval

In Tobermory Bay, Mull, lies the wreck of a Spanish Armada ship. Reputed to be carrying a cargo of gold that was supposed to be used to pay the soldiers and sailors of the Armada, the *Florida* was the scene of numerous salvage attempts. Beyond the odd coin or piece of silver plate, most of the items salvaged consisted of the detritus of everyday life on board a sailing vessel of the time. Literally thousands of pounds were spent on finding the small amount of items recovered.

hero of the War of Independence, lost his ship, the *Bonhomme Richard*, off Flamborough Head in 1779 in a ship-to-ship duel with HMS *Serapis*. He escaped in the captured *Serapis* because his own ship was so badly damaged in the battle. Although the general position of this famous battle is well known, a substantial and well-equipped expedition funded by the bestselling author Clive Cussler failed to find any trace of the ship in weeks of surveying. Sub-bottom profiling equipment which penetrates to the layer below the mud or sand on the surface of the seabed is another new survey technique which can help identify wreck sites.

Diving on wrecks became available to amateurs as well as professionals with the development of scuba-diving equipment in the 1950s. The diver carried his own air supply and was not dependent on a pipe attached to an air pump on the surface. Amateur diving is a major hobby, of which exploring wrecks is one major aspect, and many wrecks have been discovered as a result of amateur expeditions. The negative side of this new pastime has been that many have seen it as a salvaging or souvenir-hunting exercise. Non-ferrous items on recent wrecks can fetch good prices as scrap and also make good souvenirs. This does not make for good archaeology. The Nautical Archaeology Society has campaigned to educate amateur divers and has developed a series of training schemes to equip them with the correct survey and excavation techniques. On the positive side many of the successes of underwater archaeology would not have been possible without amateur volunteers.

Above: Many ships have disappeared in the oceans without any trace. For example, the magnificent Danish training ship *København* was the most modern and best equipped of its kind when launched in 1921, yet it disappeared in 1928 while on passage from Buenos Aires to Melbourne. Such vanished ships can be found even in the deepest water with modern underwater technology.

Opposite above: In sand and mud shipwrecks can be covered and uncovered very rapidly as banks are shifted. The wrecks themselves can cause obstructions which causes the current to scour out a hole round them which will eventually bury them. Wrecks can suddenly emerge after gales have shifted sandbanks. This intact, nineteenth-century, wooden, three-masted barque emerged from the sands on the north bank of the Mersey estuary at Ainsdale in November 1988. Within a year, it had all but disappeared again.

Opposite below: On the other hand, some shipwrecks remain on the shore. The rocky shore of Kelp Lagoon on East Falkland contains this massive fragment of the American ship *St Mary.* It was lost on its maiden voyage in 1890 and was one of the last examples of the 'Downeaster'. In 1978, a section of its timbers was recovered, conserved and displayed at the Maine State Museum.

The *Mary Rose* project incorporated thousands of hours of amateur diving time. Amateur divers have also helped in seabed surveys for larger areas such as the surveys carried out by the Hampshire and Isle of Wight Archaeological Trust in the Solent. Given the huge number of wrecks that litter our coast, there is certainly a need to survey and identify the most important sites. This has been carried out on land over many years and has resulted in the 'scheduling' of about 10,000 ancient monuments such as barrows, ritual circles and fortifications. The Protection of Wrecks Act of 1973 has so far extended to just under eighty sites around the British coast. But policing such sites is difficult. There is a licensing system to permit divers to work particular sites and there is a supervisory diving team who make a regular round of visits to monitor the individual sites. Responsibility for the underwater archaeological heritage within the twelve-mile territorial limit has recently been transferred to English Heritage to bring it into line with the land-based heritage. This may mean that greater resources could become available to carry out surveys and systematic excavations.

Nevertheless there are many threats to historic shipwrecks from the commercial exploitation of the seabed, including sand and gravel dredging, offshore installations for the oil and gas industry and commercial salvage operations.

This is also the case for shipwrecks worldwide. For example, the demands from the antiques trade for Classical sculpture or ceramics have seen the looting of Greek and Roman wrecks in the Mediterranean. At the same time, the techniques for exploring the deep waters of the world have become more and more sophisticated. Research for the offshore oil industry and for the major navies has seen the development of deep-diving manned submersibles and ROVs (remotely operated vehicles) which can recover material from the depths. The recovery of fittings and personal items from the wreck of the *Titanic*, starting from two miles below the surface by an ROV, shows how sophisticated these remotely controlled 'submarines' have become. After many years of diplomacy, 2002 saw the launching of a UNESCO Convention to lay down guidelines to protect the world's underwater archaeological heritage. But not all countries have signed up to it and many poorer nations do not have the resources to police such regulations. They may also consider the exploitation of valuable shipwrecks as a useful means of increasing their revenues. It is also difficult to enforce such regulations on the high seas and there will have to be some compromises made between the demands for systematic archaeological excavation and the commercial requirements of salvage companies.

CHAPTER SEVEN

LEFT TO ROT:
BURIED AND BEACHED SHIPS

Underwater archaeology can be spectacular, deploying the latest technology and attracting huge publicity. You only have to think back to the excitement caused by Bob Ballard's discovery of the wreck of the *Titanic* and the continuing grip that wreck has on the public imagination. The study of the remains of vessels beached and abandoned on the shore or buried in mud does not have the same glamour. Yet these humble remains can yield much information about the both distant and recent past histories of ships, boats and people.

There are many reasons why a vessel is abandoned by its owners. It may be because of lack of work, or it could be because the owners have gone bankrupt. The ship itself may be out of date or perhaps require major and unaffordable repairs. There may also be no other means of getting rid of it. If it is built of wood, it may not be worth breaking up. This can also be the case for a metal-hulled vessel if it ends up in a remote part of the world far from the markets for scrap metal. There are also owners who are sentimentally attached to a vessel and cannot bear to see it broken up even though it has outlived its usefulness. Equally there are owners, especially boat owners, who fall out of love with their craft or who become too ill to sail them. The result is the same: without care and attention the vessel will rot away.

Ships deteriorate from the day of their launch. They are afloat in a hostile medium, the sea, which can batter the hull with huge force. The motion of the waves can leave a hull without support as it makes its passage, causing racking and straining. Water will find its way into any chink and aperture of a hull. It can mount a chemical or electrolytic attack and sea creatures within it can make their own assault. Unless maintenance is carried out regularly and conscientiously, hulls will leak, rot or rust and such weakness will cause sinking or leave the vessel useless, fit only for scrapping or abandonment. The process does not stop there. Often all that eventually remains of a ship that has been left to rot is the lower parts of the hull which have been enfolded by the preserving qualities of anaerobic mud.

Above: The *Jhelum* lies at the upper end of Stanley Harbour and was once the Packe family's workshop and wool store. It was last in use in the 1960s as a petrol store. The stern section is well protected with corrugated iron but was set on fire in 1982 and the dark burn marks are still visible. The bow section is beginning to distort and many planks are missing on the wind and waterline.

Opposite above: The *Jhelum*'s interior aft is still in excellent condition. It was constructed of the best-quality timber including deck beams of African mahogany and these have retained huge residual strength because they and their iron fastenings have been protected from rot and rust by the corrugated-iron roof.

Opposite middle: The unprotected section of the *Jhelum* is a complete contrast; most of the main and 'tween deck beams have rotted through and this will lead to the collapse of the side frames and planking. The cutting of a large aperture through the middle of the ship was to allow goods to be carried along the jetty from the shore or lifted out of a schooner tied up alongside and this has also weakened the structure of the hull.

Opposite below: The waves are driven by the prevailing wind which often reaches gale force directly into the *Jhelum*'s starboard bow. Over the course of time they have loosened the fastenings of the outer planks and these have become detached. This has exposed the frames of the ship to wave action. They in turn will collapse along the wind and waterline and bring down the upper section of the bow to be attacked in its turn. In the end there will be nothing left of the hull above the water.

Since 1998 greater activity by marine boring molluscs has been detected in Stanley Harbour. In 2002 teredo, which bore large holes down the grain of the wood, and gribble, which make small holes, were found in the *Jhelum's* timbers. They will hasten the collapse of the hull. This close-up of a sample of infected planking shows how damaging the combined activities of teredo and gribble can be.

The 428-ton wooden barque *Jhelum* is a good example of what can happen. It was built in Liverpool in 1849 by a reputable firm of shipbuilders, Joseph Steel & Son, and they traded it on their own account until 1863. It made many hard voyages to the west coast of South America until it entered Stanley Harbour, East Falkland on 18 August 1869, carrying a cargo of guano and was leaking badly. The owners refused to answer for the ship and the unfortunate master, John Beaglehole, was left with no money and the responsibility for the ship. After almost two years of wrangling, which even involved the Duke of Edinburgh (captain of the visiting warship HMS *Galatea*), Beaglehole was able to quit his ship. The *Jhelum* was sold for use as a wool store and workshop and beached in the upper harbour. Its forward end was left uncovered and the stern was fitted with a corrugated-iron roof. The roof has kept the stern section in a remarkable state of preservation, but the bow section has gradually collapsed. Rainwater has penetrated the deck beams and upper frames and they have rotted and collapsed. The process has been speeded up by roosting seabirds, whose droppings have fertilised crevices, and windblown seeds from the land have germinated in these. These in turn created more pockets of dampness for fungal spores to do their work in degrading the timbers. The ship is fastened with a mixture of wooden dowels called treenails, iron nails and copper bolts, all of which are deteriorating in their different ways, and the result is that many of the planks have been loosened and have floated off. This has exposed the frames behind them, which ensure the structural integrity of the hull. The loss of the planking means that the frames are battered by waves whipped up by the frequent local gales. They will eventually collapse along the wind and waterline and thereby expose another section of the hull to the same treatment. In recent years, the process has been accelerated by the arrival of marine boring worms – teredo and gribble – in the timbers.

Their activities riddle the wood with holes and reduce its strength. Eventually all that will be left is the keel and the floor timbers sunk in the sand.

The types of deterioration – fungal rot, metal oxidation and environmental battering – recorded on the *Jhelum* over the last twenty years have been at work on abandoned vessels down the ages. Yet even in their rotted state, wooden derelicts can contain a great deal of information about their construction, the people who used them and the circumstances of their abandonment. These can be revealed through systematic archaeological excavation. This has been amply demonstrated by the many discoveries around the British Isles, ranging from a fragment of a plank to fairly complete hulls.

Old boats have been discovered as a result of excavations for some other purpose. Such discoveries go back before the time when systematic archaeology was practised. As long ago as 1667, Samuel Pepys recorded the discovery of the remains of a 500-ton Elizabethan galleon during excavations to extend the quay space at Deptford Dockyard. He mentioned this as a curiosity. There was no question of taking measurements and recording the remains. In 1822, a complete medieval vessel was dug up during drainage operations on the Kent marshes at New Romney. This was fully recorded and published in the proceedings of the Society of Antiquaries. The nineteenth century witnessed a rapid growth in interest in the study of the past, and the excavation of ancient monuments grew apace. Local museums with archaeological collections were established; scholarly archaeological and historical societies were set up and excavation reports were published. Most of the work was on land, but there were also reports on boat discoveries. Just like Pepys' galleon, they were chance discoveries. For example, the dredging of the Manchester Ship Canal from 1893 has brought up a number of log boats in the Warrington area which were reported in the proceedings of the Warrington Literary and Philosophical Society. Many other examples of log boats have been dug up all around the British Isles. Many of the initial reports suggested that these must be prehistoric because of their primitive construction from large single oak trees. However, archaeology has made huge advances in the last fifty years. Radiocarbon dating and tree ring analysis are scientific techniques which can provide reasonably accurate dates for wooden structures. Some log boats, such as the ones at Warrington, have been tested and found to have been built in the Anglo-Saxon and early medieval periods.

There have been many log boat finds and this is partly due to the stout character of these craft. Discoveries of later craft have not been so numerous, but a single find can throw a whole new light on shipping developments in a particular era. The boats found in the muddy shore of the Humber at North Ferriby in the late 1930s revealed one way in which a log boat became extended into a multi-planked boat, with a central keel plank, side planks and raised sides all sewn together with twisted branches of yew. A piece of the same type of boat at Caldicot and a fairly complete boat at Dover have been excavated in 1990 and 1992. Both date from the Bronze Age and show that this type of construction was not unique to the Humber. The size of the Dover boat also suggests that it was used for cross-Channel trading. The older of the two boats, from Llyn Peris, shows us that there were other ways of building a

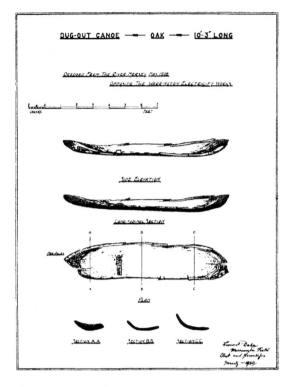

DUG-OUT CANOE ─── OAK ─── 10'-3" LONG

Left: Log boats (as they are called today) or dug-out canoes have been found in large numbers in dredging and waterside excavations. With the exception of the boat found in the Kent marshes in 1822, they were the first buried boats to be investigated archaeologically. There was usually no one who had knowledge of naval architecture to write up their excavation and as a result the older reports tend to lack detail. This example of an early report on log boats was prepared in 1909.

Below left: The discovery of this boat in Llyn Peris, North Wales is important because it shows how some of the early boatbuilders tackled the transition from a single dugout to a proper hull with built-up sides. This still has a single hollowed log for the bottom section of its hull but with raised sides made from separate planks.

Opposite: The Sutton Hoo ship was buried deliberately as part of the ritual of interring an exceptionally important person in early seventh-century Anglo-Saxon England. The ship, which was 88 feet long and 15 feet wide, had to be dragged up a steep slope from the River Deben near Woodbridge to this high ground which formed a cemetery. The ship was stowed with a fine array of treasure to go with the dead man into the after life. The high bow and stern were probably left projecting out of the mound of earth that covered the ship.

boat, as it has a bottom fashioned from a single timber with raised side planking to give it greater capacity and water capability. This fragment dates from medieval times and this demonstrates that there is no continuous line of design development. Old and tried techniques were retained where they were still fit for their purpose.

The single most important boat find must be the Sutton Hoo ship, not just because it was a ship from the early Anglo-Saxon period, but because of its contents. It was a ship that was deliberately buried as part of a religious ritual. It housed the mortal remains of a king, probably Raedwald, who died about 625 and who had been overlord of all the Anglo-Saxon kingdoms south of the Humber. The king, as befitted his status, needed to be accompanied with symbols of his power and prestige during his earthly life. The ship itself was part of this expression, for it was over 88 feet long and capable of carrying twenty oarsmen on either side. The central section contained the body, which had disappeared in the acid sandy soil, and a fabulous array of jewellery and weapons. The ship's wooden frames and clinker planking had rotted away, but the sand carried their impression as well as containing the rivets that fastened the hull. The vessel and its hoard was first discovered in 1939 and the onset of war meant that the excavations had to be suspended for the duration. The priority had been the recovery of the treasures and the ship, or rather its shadow in the sand, was considered of lesser importance. The most important drawings of the ship were unfortunately destroyed in the war and it was not until 1965 that the archaeologists could return to the site.

Above: The British Isles have not yielded many significant finds of ships dating from the Middle Ages. The European side of the North Sea and the Baltic has seen the discovery of a wealth of ship finds. The Dutch polder lands have been progressively reclaimed from the Zuider Zee and these new farmlands have seen many excavations of wrecked and abandoned ships, including this large thirteenth-century Kogge in 1983. Ships' timbers of this period were so plentiful in this area that the archaeologists were burning the timbers after drawing and measuring them.

In the intervening period between 1939 and 1965 there had been a growing recognition of the importance of studying the archaeology of ancient ships. The publication of an article on the North Ferriby boats in 1947 was an indicator. The reconstruction of the Sutton Hoo ship after the war had led to more discoveries, such as the Roman ship uncovered at Blackfriars, London in 1962. But perhaps the event that brought shore-based maritime archaeology to general recognition among archaeologists and maritime historians was the discovery of the remains of a late-Saxon vessel at Graveney in 1970. It brought together a team drawn from the British Museum and the National Maritime Museum and it resulted in the preservation of its timbers and an assessment by a naval architect of the vessel's stability characteristics and its likely performance under sail. This approach has become highly developed in Scandinavia, where major ship discoveries from the same period, especially the Skuldelev ships in 1962, led to conservation and display, followed by the construction of replicas to test the performance of the original vessels.

Further discoveries of ancient ships have continued. The coastline of the Bristol Channel has proved to be fruitful, with the discovery of a Romano-Celtic ship of the third century at Barlands Farm, Gwent in 1993. In 1994, the remains of a medieval ship from the eleventh or twelfth century was found at Magor Pill and in 2002 a very large fifteenth-century ship was found in the bank of the River Usk at Newport. This is possibly the most important of the recent discoveries. At the moment the main priority is to ensure that the local authorities agree to the fullest recovery of the hull and to find funds for its conservation. There have also been many other finds of small reused ship's timbers. The medieval area of the port of London has been especially productive, with ships' timbers – including the remains of ships of the thirteenth century – discovered among the remains of timber wharves.

Our knowledge of more recent types of ships can also be improved by the study of cast-off remains. The coastline of the British Isles has a wide range of tidal conditions affected, for example, by exposure to the Atlantic, a prevailing wind or the nature of the coast, whether sandy and shallow or rocky and deep. The home port can also be widely varied, from a deepwater harbour with water at all states of the tide, to a shallow estuary with a high rise and fall in the tide or a beach as a landing place without the shelter of a harbour. On top of these variations there are the different local cultures which have also seen differences of approach to boat design. So, for example, a boat for netting salmon on a tidal estuary differed in design and construction depending on where it originated. A salmon boat on the River Dee, therefore, was a broad, shallow, clinker-built boat, about 17 feet long and just over 6 feet wide, with a flat (transom) stern for paying out the long seine net.

The salmon punt on the River Severn uses a similar net but is shaped like a punt, with a flat bottom and flat ends, and is over 20 feet long by only 3 feet 6 inches wide. This rich variety of designs can be seen in other ships with the same purpose. There was a need to transport heavy bulk cargoes such as stone, grain and coal and to take lighter cargoes from deep sea ships to warehousing or factories inland from a port. The design of barges for such traffic evolved in very different ways, thus the Mersey flat was different from the Severn trow, which in turn was different from the Humber keel or the Thames barge. The knowledge of how to design and build all these many types of working boats was usually passed down by word of mouth, from master shipwright to his apprentices. There were usually no plans involved.

The early twentieth century saw the disappearance of many of these types. There were no Severn trows or Mersey flats sailing by the middle of the twentieth century; competition from road transport and the decline of British industry robbed them of their purpose. Sailing fishing boats followed a similar pattern of steep decline. At Lowestoft, for example, thirty-three sailing trawlers were built in the years immediately after the First World War and the local fleet still numbered 124 in 1930. By 1939 there were only eight left. The others had been abandoned and left to rot, with a few sold abroad or motorised.

This rapid decline, and in some cases extinction, of local traditional boats galvanised a few interested people to record what remained. The late Edgar March, who went on to write the standard works on sailing trawlers, drifters and Thames barges, recalled the jolt that seeing the sad sight of abandoned fishing trawlers gave him:

Above: In the twentieth century many traditional types of wooden sailing ship disappeared. They were displaced by powered vessels, the lack of work in the depression of the interwar years and simply by wearing out in old age. Most, like these two fishing smacks abandoned in Southwold Harbour, Suffolk, were stripped of anything useful and then left to rot.

Opposite above left: Once the decks come off and there is no maintenance, a wooden hull soon breaks down. This is a recently abandoned ship's lifeboat that had been converted into a motor fishing vessel on the north coast of Wales. The vessel has sunk and is flooded at every tide, the wheelhouse has collapsed into the bilges and the starboard side planking has come away from the stempost.

Opposite above right: The next series of photographs are a series of before and after pictures which reinforce the point of how quickly vessels deteriorate once abandoned. The *Eustace Carey* was a jigger flat with two masts instead of the usual single one and this picture was taken when it had been newly finished at Clare & Ridgway's yard at Sankey Bridges in 1905. It was intended for carrying limestone from quarries on the North Wales coast to Fleetwood.

Opposite below: This is all that remained of the *Eustace Carey* in 2001. It remained under sail into the 1920s and then it was stripped of its masts and was converted into a towed dumb barge. About thirty years later it was no longer fit for this work and on a high tide it was floated up on to the shore at Widnes. The *Eustace Carey* remained in a fairly intact condition into the 1960s until some local arsonist burned it down to the waterline. Vegetation has covered most of what remains of it.

On Sunday the 13th October, 1946, I walked in drizzling rain round the banks of
Lake Lothing (Lowestoft). The graveyard was a depressing sight with gaunt ribs sticking
out of the mud where hulls had rotted away, others still bore the resemblance to smacks...
I turned away more determined than ever to record something of the old sailing trawlers...

The same spirit inspired the late Dr Frank Howard to do the same for Mersey flats. In the 1960s he found that almost nothing had been written about them and that the best model of one had been destroyed in the bombing of Liverpool Museum in 1941. He therefore looked round to see whether any hulks of flats survived and found the *Bedale* on the marshes near Runcorn and the *Sir R. Peel* abandoned in the mud of Widnes West Bank Dock. He measured both virtually single-handed, and that was no light task with wooden vessels over 60 feet long encased in foul-smelling mud. He used his measurements to draw up a full set of plans and from these built two scale models – one for the Science Museum and one for the Boat Museum, Ellesmere Port. Shortly after he finished his fieldwork, the *Bedale* was burned and the *Sir R. Peel* was buried. Without his dedication, our knowledge of these local barges would have been sketchy indeed.

Today, archaeology is seen as having a much wider remit than ever before and this includes the rotted remains of old ships. Planning applications for new developments on the waterfront usually call for an assessment of whether there is likely to be any significant archaeological remains. Whitewall Creek off the River Medway had been a waterway with quays for various industries, including a brick works and a chalk quarry, in the nineteenth century. As these were closed in the twentieth century it became a place for abandoning worn-out Thames barges, lighters and other craft. The first to be laid to rot there was probably the sailing barge *Milton* in 1937. Many sailing barges had not been maintained during the Second World War, and they were also seen as slow and old fashioned. As a result many were left to rot in tidal creeks all around the Thames and Medway. In the end, Whitewall Creek accommodated some eighty abandoned vessels. In the 1990s, there was a need for a new link between the north and south banks of the Medway. This was to be a tunnel, but the approach roads on the north side required the filling in of this creek. The importance of recording this assemblage of rotting hulks was recognised by the Royal Commission for Historical Monuments of England and it commissioned an experienced team to carry out a survey. While the hulks at Whitewall Creek are not unique and it cannot be argued that they are all of huge historic importance – many estuaries and abandoned basins contain the remains of old wooden vessels that have been quietly abandoned – at least they should be recorded before they are destroyed. Fortunately archaeology of all kinds has become a subject of growing fascination for the general public and this embraces not just the Roman or the Anglo-Saxon craft but old boats of more recent times. Forty years ago, for example, a group of rotting barges in a canal dock in Chester would have been summarily cut up and burned. In 2001, British Waterways, who were the site developers, employed a team of archaeologists not only to investigate them but to save the bow and stern of the oldest for preservation at the Boat Museum, Ellesmere Port. There are still other discoveries to be made.

The topsail schooner *Fanny Crosfield* is a similar case to the *Eustace Carey*. This beautiful vessel was still trading in the 1930s and has been photographed at anchor off Belfast with the last White Star liner, the *Georgic*, passing.

The *Fanny Crosfield* had been launched in 1880 at Carrickfergus for James Fisher & Co. of Barrow in Furness. It came to die at Ringneil quay on Strangford Lough and, if it had not been pointed out, there is little or no evidence on the surface of the mud to show where it rotted away.

At the time of writing, there is a newspaper report on the discovery of the remains of HMS *Beagle* in the Essex marshes. It was a naval sloop, brig rigged, of 235 tons, launched at Woolwich Dockyard in 1820. HMS *Beagle*'s claim to fame was the round-the-world voyage it undertook between 1831 and 1836. The scientist Charles Darwin sailed with it and the data he collected was the most important contribution to his theory of evolution. After its sailing days were over it became a watch vessel for the coastguard as part of the government's campaign to stop smuggling. By 1870, it was no longer fit to be a stationary depot ship and was sold to some local people for £525. The chances are that some of the upper timbers were removed and the lower part of the hull was simply towed to an outlying stretch of tidal creek and abandoned.

It is not just ancient ships that are left to rot; it is a continuing problem. Many of the world's ships are registered with what are known as 'flags of convenience'. This includes states such as Panama, Liberia and Malta. There are about forty of these flags, where the state usually licenses a commercial company to collect the fees and does not ask too many questions about the condition of the ship. This enables the owners to operate often sub-standard vessels and recruit the cheapest of crews and generally keep their costs to a minimum. If the ship is arrested while in port, then the owners, who often hide behind a screen of different companies and hirers, will often walk away leaving the ship and its crew. This happens for example, when a

There are many isolated marshes and creeks on British estuaries where old wooden vessels have been laid to rest. Purton on the Severn estuary is notable for the large number of remains of Severn trows. The *Harriet* is among the most intact and it was a 'wich barge'. This was a sub-type of trow that traded exclusively in salt from Droitwich.

These Mersey flats belonged to the Bridgewater department of the Manchester Ship Canal Co. They carried cargoes between Liverpool and Manchester and used the Bridgewater Canal rather than the main ship canal. They were towed and not sailed. After the Second World War many had worn out and were replaced by steel barges. The wooden craft had their decks lifted off and were then dumped to fill in obsolete basin and locks. Fortunately the late Jack Parkinson was able to photograph them before they were buried.

surveyor for the country in which the ship is berthed comes on board and finds safety defects such as lack of lifesaving or firefighting equipment. He can detain the ship and demand that the defects are rectified before it is allowed to sail again. There have been many cases where this has happened. In the United Kingdom there are on average about fifty cases of detaining ships a year. Of course, not all result in the owners doing 'a runner'. Sometimes it is the case that the owners have become bankrupt and the creditors have the ship arrested as a tangible asset. This is still carried out by fixing a writ from the Admiralty Court to the mast of the arrested ship. For example, the Nigeria Line, which was one of a number of symbols of the country's newly granted independence from Britain in the 1960s, ran out of money in the troubled 1980s and this left one ship and its unlucky crew high and dry at Ellesmere Port on the Manchester Ship Canal for almost three years. The crew were not paid and had no money to fly home and in the end had to depend on food and supplies from organisations such as the Missions to Seamen. The vessel went for scrap and this contemporary episode is not so different from the story of the *Jhelum* and poor Captain Beaglehole and his crew back in 1871.

Top: The archaeological heritage of old abandoned craft has been treated more seriously in recent years. When British Waterways wanted to develop an old filled-in basin at Chester in 2001, they paid the cost for a team of archaeologists to record the remains of the Mersey flats buried there. The oldest proved to go back to 1801 and its bow and stern were dug up and taken to the Boat Museum, Ellesmere Port for preservation.

Above: Steel ships can also deteriorate rapidly. This is one of a small fleet of river excursion steamers that used to ply on the River Yare and on the Norfolk Broads. This is a picture from their heyday in the 1920s. They continued sailing until the 1960s.

Top: This second picture shows the shocking condition of the last survivor. This was photographed at Pin Mill on the River Orwell in 1899. The funnel and the superstructure are missing and the hull is nothing but a mass of rust.

Above: The *Royal Iris* was a Mersey ferry which could also be used for excursions and evening events. Its design was very futuristic in 1951 and it was a distinctive part of the River Mersey scene until it was pensioned off in the early 1990s. It was converted into a nightclub and was unsuccessful at several ports before ending up abandoned and rusting on the Thames in 1999. A candidate for sinking or the scrapyard if ever there was one.

Top: The Maltese-registered cargo ship *Flair* was typical of the relatively modern ships that have been abandoned by their owners. It lay in Langton Dock, Liverpool in the early 1990s. Its final destination was almost certainly the scrapyard. The crew were abandoned without wages by the owners and they ended up relying on local charities for food.

Above: This sunken wreck will never be raised or explored; it is just too dangerous. The Liberty ship *Richard Montgomery* – a standard wartime design of cargo steamer – sank in the entrance of the Medway during the Second World War loaded with ammunition.

CHAPTER EIGHT

HERITAGE SHIPS

Most ships are broken up, wrecked, sunk or destroyed in some other fashion. A few are converted to new uses, some operational and some static. An even smaller number are preserved for posterity. The reasons for preserving old ships are varied. Historic ships can be symbols of national pride or memorials to naval wars or heroes. They can be saved because of their technical importance or because of their extreme age and rarity. They can be unique experimental ships or representatives of a particular type of vessel. Quite often, the preserved ship will be the last of its kind, and can be preserved for sentimental or nostalgic reasons, perhaps on the part of seafarers who have served aboard. Equally it can be for commercial reasons, for example to enhance a new waterfront development. Aesthetics also enters into the equation. Perhaps this is why so many sailing ships have been preserved. Quite often it is a combination of some or all of these reasons. Then there are the key decisions as to whether the ship to be preserved is to be kept operating or left stationary, as well as the follow-up question as to whether the stationary ship should be left afloat or brought ashore, and if brought ashore whether or not the new berth should be covered.

Preserving ships had not been seen as a realistic proposition before the late twentieth century. Most of the famous ships of earlier times have not survived. Ships were used and then discarded with few exceptions. Brunel's *Great Eastern* went for scrap after a humiliating final few years as a public funfair, and not one of the great British battleships of the Dreadnought era was saved. The earliest example of ship preservation was probably Sir Francis Drake's *Golden Hind*. Drake made his circumnavigation in this ship between 1577 and 1580. On his return he was knighted on board the ship by Queen Elizabeth at Deptford Dockyard and his ship was placed in a special dry dock to commemorate his exploit. The public were allowed to go on board in return for a small admission fee which went to charity. The dockyard authorities had no funds for its maintenance and it eventually fell apart. After this it was many years before any other major ship was preserved in Great Britain.

There are a number of smaller boats that have been preserved from the eighteenth century. These include the magnificent royal barges which were in active use up until

The tea clipper *Cutty Sark* has been restored in all its splendour in its purpose-built dry dock at Greenwich. It was a famous ship long before it was preserved. This photograph was taken in Birkenhead Docks in 1914 when it was under the Portuguese flag. While there are many sailing ships still in the port, the official Mersey Docks and Harbour Board photographer singled the *Cutty Sark* out because of its fame.

the reign of George V and which are preserved by the National Maritime Museum. At a more mundane level the little schooner *Peggy*, dating back to about 1790, was left laid up and forgotten about in its bricked-in boathouse at Castletown on the Isle of Man, after its owner's death. It was not rediscovered until the 1930s. Today it still lies in its original berth and the house above has been converted into the Manx Nautical Museum.

The first major ship to be actively preserved was Lord Nelson's flagship at the Battle of Trafalgar, HMS *Victory*. *Victory* had a special significance because the battle not only removed the French threat of invasion, but because Nelson, the nation's naval hero, also died during that battle. It was quite an old ship in 1805, having been launched at Chatham in 1765. It continued to act as a flagship for the rest of the Napoleonic War and right on up to 1835. Admirals competed to fly their flags in it, such was its prestige. *Victory* remained a flagship for the commander-in-chief at Portsmouth, berthed at a permanent mooring. By the beginning of the twentieth century it had undergone no more than routine maintenance and was deteriorating to the point where breaking up seemed to be inevitable. In 1908 it was badly damaged when HMS *Neptune*, another wooden wall being towed off for scrap, collided with it. King Edward VII intervened to ensure it was repaired. By 1922, it was clear that the *Victory* could not stay afloat for many more years and a public appeal – the Save the *Victory* Fund – was started by Sir Geoffrey Callendar. It attracted a large donation from the ship-owner Sir James Caird, along with many smaller amounts which paid for it to be restored and permanently dry-docked. Today it remains the flagship of the Royal Navy. The repair programme has continued year in, year out with a permanent dockyard team attending to it. There has been a major effort to lighten the pressure on the ageing hull by replacing the masts with steel ones which go to the bottom of the dock and replacing the heavy cast-iron guns with lighter replicas. Many of the timbers have had to be replaced; for example, in recent years much of the bow and stern had to be rebuilt. There is probably no more than about ten percent of the original ship left, yet for any visitor going aboard it remains an evocative reminder of the days of Nelson and the sailing Navy. But as long as the *Victory* remains out in the elements it will continue to deteriorate and perhaps the only long-term solution is to enclose it in a canopy.

The question of how to retain the original structure of historic ships is a matter of great concern and debate among maritime curators responsible for such ships. If the ship is allowed to continue sailing, it is inevitable that parts of the original structure will deteriorate to the point where they will have to be replaced. A further question is how far do you go in adding extra equipment, such as an engine, propeller or radar, to make the vessel as safe as possible but without compromising its appearance? For example, the harbour tug *Brocklebank* is preserved in operating condition. Although of relatively recent build, having been launched by Yarwoods in Northwich in 1964, much of its working equipment is over thirty years old and wearing out. So, for example, the radar set that was on the ship when it was purchased in 1989 had to be changed for a modern one. This was because *Brocklebank* makes long coastal voyages to maritime festivals such as those at Portsmouth and Brest. It also had to be fitted with a GPS system and an up-to-date radio with an emergency signal. Last year the original turbo-blower which supplies high-pressure air to the eight-cylinder diesel engine was completely worn out – after spinning round at over 17,000rpm since 1964. Without it the engines could still work but only provide enough power for a speed of 3 knots. The problem was that the original makers had been taken over and such parts were difficult to find and very expensive. There was a real possibility that the *Brocklebank* would have to become a stationary preservation project. Fortunately a replacement was donated by the current suppliers. The original items have been saved in the museum's store and the installation of the new equipment photographed to create a record of these changes.

Later efforts to save historic ships have largely depended on the efforts and enthusiasm of individuals or small groups. There was little government support until the Heritage Lottery Fund was set up. It was sometimes a matter of mobilising public opinion, or, as in the case of Sir James Caird, having the funds to make salvation possible. The tea clipper *Cutty Sark* of 1869 represented one of the high points of sailing ship design. It was very strongly built with a composite hull comprising a wrought-iron keel and frames with wooden outer planking.

Left: The Maritime Trust was formed in 1970 with the aim to restore and display a representative selection of ships that had importance to British maritime history. Their first acquisition was the topsail schooner *Kathleen and May* built at Connah's Quay in 1900 and which was restored and displayed at Sutton Harbour, Plymouth.

Below: There is always a dilemma for the ship preserver between keeping as much of the original structure of the vessel and rebuilding it to get it back into a seaworthy sailing condition. This motor vessel on the slipway was once the 400-ton, three-masted barque *Elissa* built in 1877 at Aberdeen. Its stout, wrought-iron hull meant that it underwent a series of conversions, finally ending up as a cigarette-smuggling motor ship in Greek waters.

The *Elissa* was saved from the breaker's yard by the maritime archaeologist, the late Peter Throckmorton. He was able to interest the Galveston Historical Society in it and they undertook a complete and painstaking restoration over several years. This involved replacing about two thirds of the hull plating and fabricating new masts and deck fittings as well as training a crew of volunteers to actually sail it. Although it is chiefly a dockside exhibit, the *Elissa* does go to sea regularly and has undertaken long-distance voyages. As this photographs shows, it is one of the most beautiful vessels afloat.

Iron hulls were believed to make the fragrant China tea cargoes 'sweat' and deteriorate, and the whole point of a tea clipper was to deliver the new crop first and in a prime condition. After eight voyages in the tea trade, it was forced out by steamers and then made regular voyages to Australia until 1894. These made its reputation as a fast sailer. For example, the *Cutty Sark* took only sixty-nine days to sail from Newcastle, New South Wales to Land's End. It was then sold to the Portuguese, who kept it sailing for another twenty-seven years. In 1922, it was forced to put into Falmouth for shelter while on passage from London to Lisbon. Although the name had been changed and its rig altered, it was recognised by Captain Wilfred Dowman, a retired sailing ship master, and he bought it for £3,750 and restored the original rig. In 1938, it was transferred to the Thames to be part of the Thames Nautical College. After the end of the Second World War it was still in sound condition and, thanks largely to the enthusiasm of Frank Carr, the then director of the National Maritime Museum, it was preserved in a specially constructed dry dock on the Greenwich waterfront. The *Cutty Sark* remains there to this day, but, even as one of the most 'iconic' pieces of Britain's maritime heritage, its future cannot be taken for granted. Although it has always been well maintained – and this has included installing new masts – it is a huge object to look after in a hostile environment. Apart from the 200-foot-high masts, and their six spars and their miles of rigging, there are hundreds of feet of wooden deck planks. The gaps between these have to be caulked with oakum and pitch to make the deck waterproof. The hull itself lies within the damp atmosphere of its 'dry dock'. A recent report by the director of the *Cutty Sark* Trust stated:

> The strength of the ship's composite construction, a mixture of wood and iron, is the reason for her survival, but the method of construction is now causing serious problems. The build-up of rust at the faying surfaces between wood and iron, and iron and iron, is forcing the hull apart. The rust is causing rivets to sheer and the yellow metal bolts to fail and the very damp British atmosphere doesn't help either. So the wrought-iron frame of the ship's composite hull is rusting, and if this deterioration continues unchecked the ship's future is at risk.

Several years ago I remember being shown the keelson, the girder that runs along the centre line of the ship from stem to stern above the frames. Rust was clearly active and there were holes in the upright sections. Although wrought iron is a tough material and the *Cutty Sark* was built with the best quality to the thickest specification, nevertheless age is taking its toll. A major refit is needed and the estimated cost is not less than £8 million. However income, which is mainly from admissions, is falling. Even a famous vessel like this finds it difficult to attract enough visitors. There is huge competition for tourists' money in the London area, which has seen an overall decline in tourism since 11 September. However, at the time of writing the *Cutty Sark's* trustees are preparing a bid for funding from the Heritage Lottery Fund.

The third most famous of all British preserved ships must be the *Great Britain*. I do not count the *Mary Rose*, Henry VIII's battleship which was raised from the Solent in 1983, as there is no more than half the hull left and it must be regarded as an archaeological object rather than an intact historic ship. The *Great Britain*, which has already been mentioned in chapter four, was abandoned as a wool storage hulk in the Falklands in 1933. As there was no local market for scrap, it was towed out to Sparrow Cove in the outer harbour at Stanley to get it out of the way. It was salvaged and brought back to Bristol in 1971. As with the *Cutty Sark*, there were a number of enthusiastic and influential individuals who worked very hard to bring this to pass, including Dr (now Reverend) Ewen Corlett, a distinguished naval architect whose letter to the *Times* in 1967 about its possible salvage proved to be such a catalyst; the late Dr Basil Greenhill, the then director of the National Maritime Museum; Richard Goold Adams, who financed the feasibility survey and who became the first chairman of the *Great Britain* Trust; and Sir Jack Hayward, who paid for the German salvage team to go and rescue the ship.

Left: The authentic replica of Captain Cook's exploration ship *Endeavour* is one way in which maritime heritage can be perpetuated. It is one of several ambitious reconstructions of extinct types of sailing vessel which include a seventeenth-century Dutch East Indiaman, the *Batavia*, and an early eighteenth-century Swedish East India Co. ship launched in 2003.

Below: The *Carrick*, ex-*City of Adelaide*, of 1864 has a composite hull like the *Cutty Sark* and beautiful lines. Unfortunately the Scottish Maritime Museum does not have the funds to look after it, but there is a possibility that it might be taken to Adelaide for preservation.

The *Great Britain* back in its building dock at Bristol, restored to its original appearance. Plans are in hand to build a glazed 'sea' around the top wall of the dock to allow the major part of the hull to be dehumidified to slow down the rusting of the frames and plates.

Once the *Great Britain* was safely back in its original building dock in Bristol, the process of restoration could begin and, apart from tidying up the neglected hull, there were major decisions to be made about its appearance. Was it to be restored as its last use – a three-masted sailing ship – or as a three-masted auxiliary steamer on the Australian run, or as Brunel's original transatlantic liner with five masts? As there was nothing left of the later engines and cabins, the sensible choice was to revert back to the original revolutionary appearance. This then determined the rig; the three wooden masts which had been installed at the time of its second rebuilding were taken out and saved. The mizzen was left in the Falklands as a monument to the *Great Britain*'s long stay in Stanley Harbour. The unique, five-masted rig was reinstated and the original hull decorations at the bow and paint scheme with dummy gunports along each side were reinstated. New decks, companionways, skylights and replicas of the iron lifeboats were all fabricated. Below, a replica of the six-bladed propeller was installed. The interior accommodation has been partially reinstated and, while the grand saloon with its elaborate mouldings and red carpet is not only an eye-catching exhibit, it earns money from being hired out for banquets and weddings. Work on recreating the huge, four-cylinder, steam engine and its chain drive to the propeller shaft is still going on. But, in thirty-two years of dry docking the huge iron hull has continued to slowly rust away. While protective paint can be applied to the outer surfaces, there are many riveted joints between parts of the frames and the hull plating that are inaccessible. The high humidity in the bottom of the dock has also helped the corrosion process. The build-up of rust is tending to force these joints apart as on the *Cutty Sark*. It is impossible to take such joints apart and so, to give the *Great Britain* a long-term future, a new conservation plan was needed. This involved the creation of a closed-in area in the dock around the hull which can be environmentally controlled. The dock will be fitted with a glazed 'roof' around the hull and dehumidifying equipment installed below it which will retard (though not reverse) the corrosion process. This will cost about £7 million! Ship preservation is never cheap and the work does not stop with the successful acquisition and restoration campaign.

Britain saw a movement to preserve ships from the 1970s. Before then very few maritime or port museums would have ever considered saving a ship. It was part of a general expansion of museums in that decade. The Imperial War Museum acquired the cruiser HMS *Belfast* and the National Museum of Wales established a new Maritime and Industrial Museum in Cardiff Docks. They bought a tug, a pilot cutter, a steam dredger and a sailing ketch. The Ulster Folk and Transport Museum bought the schooner *Result* and steam sludge tanker *Divis*. There were new maritime museums: the Scottish Maritime Museum at Irvine majored on collecting ships with a flotilla of five ships: a tug, a puffer, a tanker, a steam yacht and a large composite sailing ship, *Carrick* of 1864, while the Boat Museum at Ellesmere Port rapidly acquired a fleet of every possible variation of canal boat. The latter examples were set up not only to preserve the local maritime heritage but to help revive a derelict waterfront and to boost the local economy through tourism. Both had large amounts of capital invested in them but have had to struggle to find the running costs and this has affected the level of maintenance on their ships. So far neither have had to get rid of any of their ships, but the huge wooden and iron hull of the *Carrick*, although drawn up on a slipway, looks insupportable. In national terms it is close in design to the *Cutty Sark* and there is certainly an argument to be made for preserving only one of each kind of major vessel. Otherwise what few resources that are available will be spread too thinly. Elsewhere some ships that were 'saved' in the initial rush have had to be sold or scrapped. The Ulster Folk and Transport Museum reluctantly sold the *Divis* because they could not find the costs of restoring and moving it to their landlocked site. The Museum of Wales have dispersed their fleet, and the fleet of steamers that were assembled at Maryport as a seagoing version of the Windermere Steam Boat Museum has been sold or scrapped. Nevertheless visitors to maritime museums expect to see ships and not just relics, recordings or models of them. The problem remains that preserving a ship costs far more than any other museum conservation work and the work is never ending.

Maritime museums are not the only collectors of historic ships; there have also been associations and individuals who were also dedicated to saving old vessels. The leading body was the Maritime Trust, which was intended to do for the nation's historic ships what the National Trust had done to save stately homes and historic landscapes for posterity. The Trust took on the *Cutty Sark* and built up a fine collection, ranging from fishing boats to the steam coaster *Robin*, the topsail schooner

Kathleen and May and the Victorian naval sloop HMS *Gannet* (formerly the training ship *Mercury*). Initially the Trust's vessels were dispersed around the country so that the Yarmouth steam drifter *Lydia Eva* was based in Great Yarmouth with a loyal band of volunteers undertaking its maintenance, while the schooner *Kathleen and May*, which had been owned in the West Country, was based at Plymouth. Then it was decided to show most of the fleet together in the refurbished St Katherine's Dock in London. It seemed like an excellent location, close to the tourist route with the Tower of London and HMS *Belfast* nearby. In the event it did not work; visitors were very happy to enjoy the activity and beauty these old ships brought to the dock, but they were not sufficiently interested in paying to go on board. The Trust has had to retrench and the fleet has been dispersed to other preservation bodies. So, for example, their steam tug *Portwey* is operated from West India Dock by volunteers who have formed their own company and the *Robin*, which has lain rather neglected in the next berth, has recently been taken on by a trust purely dedicated to its welfare. The *Kathleen and May* went back west after a spell as a static exhibition ship in a new development at Southwark, and while one dedicated Bideford man has spent over £700,000 rebuilding it back to sailing condition, its future on the Torridge is still uncertain and it may well be sold to enthusiasts in Southern Ireland.

There have also been associations which have concentrated on one type of ship, and they have tended to aim at keeping the ship sailing. The Norfolk Wherry Trust was founded as long ago as 1949 to buy and sail one of the last surviving Norfolk wherries, the *Albion* of 1898. The Trust's initial aim was to keep the *Albion* earning its keep by carrying cargo. But cargoes became scarce and heavy ones, such as sugar beet, were hard on a tired hull and even caused the *Albion* to sink on one occasion in 1957. The Trust then turned to hiring it out to groups over the summer with a paid skipper in charge and this and other fund-raising has succeeded in keeping it sailing. Hiring, or more technically charter work, plus members' subscriptions and grants keeps a number of other historic ships working, such as the *Centaur* and the *Pudge*, two barges run by the Thames Barge Sailing Club. Unlike the Norfolk Wherry folk, this club is more dedicated to keeping the traditional skills of sailing these barges rather than preserving a particular one. Since their foundation in 1948, they have chartered long term or owned the following barges: *Spurgeon*, *Arrow*, *Asphodel* and *Westmorland*.

There are also dedicated groups of individuals who devote all their spare time to restoring a single boat. In 1971, a group of about a dozen steam engine enthusiasts in Liverpool decided to buy the last steam tug on the Mersey, the *Kerne*. It had been built at Montrose in 1913 and, after working at Chatham Naval Dockyard, had been

Opposite above: The trawler *Amadine* has been installed at Ostend with its hull glazed in to provide an exhibition area and access to the bottom of the hull for visitors.

Opposite below: The submarine HMS *Alliance* has been set up on a concrete platform at the Submarine Museum at Gosport. An entrance and exit has been cut through the starboard side to allow visitors into the cramped spaces of its interior.

The *Divis* of 1928 was a steam sewage sludge carrier for the Belfast Corporation, which made a daily voyage down Belfast Lough to the dumping grounds. Ulster Folk and Transport Museum tried to save this everyday steamer when it came out of service in the 1970s, but they did not have the resources to move and restore it on their land-based site. They did have the good sense to make a documentary film of it working, however, which provides an excellent record of a ship that could not be saved.

brought to the Mersey in the 1940s for towing barges. The enthusiasts formed a company – the North Western Steam Ship Co. – and gave themselves ten years to keep the ship steaming. In the event they have so far managed it for thirty-two years. There have been many hours of hard work on general maintenance and on major refits such as re-tubing the boiler. They have also added to their income by taking on the occasional film contract and making use of job creation schemes. The *Kerne*, at 75 feet long and 19 feet beam, is sufficiently small to be viable for preservation by a small group, and there are similar examples of steam tugs and VICs being preserved by individuals elsewhere. The major obstacle to long-term preservation is the cost of major repairs: the steam dredger *Seiont 2* was transferred to a local trust at Caernarfon, its home port, by the National Museum of Wales and it was maintained in steaming condition for over twenty years. But in the end it proved impossible to find the funds to carry out the hull and boiler repairs and it was sent for scrap.

Smaller fishing boats and yachts have also been revived in the hands of individual boat-owners. The Old Gaffers Association, which is for owners of gaff-rigged yachts, and the Steam Boat Association have hundreds of boats on their registers. They organise races and meetings and have newsletters to swap information and advertise the sale of boats. Individual types of fishing boats, such as cobles on the north-east coast, nobbies in North Wales and Lancashire, Brixham trawlers in Devon, Colchester oyster smacks and Cornish luggers have all seen a revival in numbers.

Another approach to ship preservation can be seen at the National Fishing Heritage Centre at Grimsby. All the details, sights, sounds and smells of a steam trawler are reconstructed inside the building, including the trawler's boiler room with the fireman stoking the boiler.

It is now possible to hold races for Brixham trawlers and Cornish luggers. The Excelsior Trust at Lowestoft has successfully bought back from Norway the Lowestoft sailing trawler *Excelsior*, which had been built in the port in 1921, and restored it to sailing. They have even taken it out trawling for a television documentary. What makes the Trust outstanding is that it has been able to buy its own ship repair yard and embark on a training scheme to pass on the skills needed to maintain traditional wooden sailing boats. They also earn income from repairing other vessels and have acquired another smack, the *William McCann* built at Hull in 1884, as a long-term rebuilding project.

There must be doubts about the long-term survival of many ships and boats in the British maritime heritage fleet. Perhaps too many are being preserved and the resources are being spread too thinly. Nevertheless new candidates for preservation are being proposed all the time and indeed many have merit. HMS *Whimbrel*, an anti-submarine frigate from the Second World War, is about to be scrapped by the Egyptian Navy, while the *Manxman*, the last of the Isle of Man Steam Packet Co.'s turbine steamers, or the last intact British passenger liner, the *Windsor Castle*, all have their merits and groups of ardent supporters. However their size and in some cases their condition tend to suggest that they can only be preserved for a limited number of years and not in perpetuity. Until the 1990s, there was no overall idea of how many historic ships were available. The National Maritime Museum set up

The paddle steamer *Waverley* has been kept afloat and in steam by the Paddle Steamer Preservation Co. since 1975. It earns its keep by carrying thousands of passengers on coastal excursions during the summer, just as it did when operated commercially on the Clyde by Caledonian MacBrayne. The *Waverley* has had several major refits to replace the boiler, for major hull repairs and to ensure it can keep its passenger certificate. These major expenses have been largely met by grants from the Heritage Lottery Fund.

the National Historic Ships Committee, which has been able to identify over a thousand vessels that could be considered historic, and this is after they limited their research to vessels over 40 feet long, or over 40 tons and built before 1945. So all the large number of fishing smacks and vintage yachts were omitted. Out of that total, they were then able to identify about fifty ships which could be considered as the core national collection and about another 200 which were significant. This has helped provide guidance to the Heritage Lottery Fund, which has been besieged for grant applications for ship and boat restoration. This has also been widely accepted as authoritative among the wider ship-preserving community, while the Committee has also been able to extend its list to some important ships built after 1945. But it cannot guarantee the future of any of the ships and many of the ships on the Core List remain at risk, including the top-ranking *Cutty Sark*.

Above: The Humber Keel and Sloop Preservation Society was founded in 1970 to restore an example of a Humber keel and a Humber sloop back to sail. Keels, rigged with a square sail on a single lowering mast, were cargo carriers on the inland sections of the Humber and its tributaries, while the sloop was gaff-rigged with a mainsail and jib and was capable of coastal voyages. The steel-hulled keel *Comrade* of 1923 was purchased in 1975, to be followed by the sloop *Amy Howson* of 1914. This Society has been very successful in keeping these two unique local barges sailing on their native waters. As with most preserved sailing vessels they are fitted with diesel engines for speeding up the process of docking.

Opposite above: The Excelsior Trust have not only preserved the *Excelsior*, one of the last Lowestoft trawlers, they have also bought a small shipyard with slipways where they can overhaul it and other heritage vessels such as the Norfolk wherry *Albion*.

Opposite below: Old skills such as wooden shipwrighting need to be preserved as well as supplies of expensive and scarce timber. Even a traditional narrowboat requires big pieces of English oak for its stempost, frames and planking. The Black Country Museum at Dudley has built a small boatyard and has had narrowboats rebuilt in the traditional way.

Previous page:

Above: A trio of preserved steamers can normally be seen at the Boat Museum, Ellesmere Port. In the foreground, the *Basuto* was built as a Clyde puffer in 1902 for carrying cargo on the Forth & Clyde Canal. It eventually became a work boat on the Manchester Ship Canal. Behind it, the steam tug *Kerne* of 1913 is kept working by its owners, while the larger tug and director's launch, the *Daniel Adamson* of 1903, has been virtually abandoned since it finished working in the 1970s.

Below: Thames barges have survived in larger numbers than any other of the local types of sailing barges. Many came out of commercial service as motor barges and were re-rigged. In August 2000, there were five berthed at St Katherine's Dock, London which earned their keep by hosting corporate parties and sailing trips. From right to left, they were the *Ardwina, Ironsides, Raybel, Gladys* and *Phoenecian*.

154

Left: Small traditional fishing boats such as the Lancashire nobbie (sometimes also called the Morecambe Bay prawner or a half-decker) make good preservation projects for individual owners. But many have been changed in appearance with raised cabins to make them more comfortable as cruising boats. This is one that has been converted back to the original layout complete with a beam trawl.

Below: Racing traditional boats such as the oyster smacks that used to work on the Kent and Essex coasts has become very popular, with the number of contestants reaching double figures. This was the start of the smacks race in Swale Regatta in 2001, which also had races for Thames barges and traditional yachts.

Top: The *Tid* tug was a standard design built in large numbers in the Second World War. At 54 tons and 74 feet long, it is of a small enough size to be suitable for restoration by an individual owner. *Tid* 172 is kept on moorings off Shotley in the Orwell estuary. The three-masted schooner in the background is a conversion from a Fairmile type of naval patrol boat.

Above: Not all preservation campaigns are successful. The paddle tug *John H. Amos* was built in 1931 for towage on the River Tees. It was acquired in the 1970s by the local museum for preservation. Budget reductions forced a sale to a private owner who took the tug to Chatham. Unfortunately the tug sank and has since been dragged out on to an adjacent slipway. Recently a trust has been set up to save this important little ship.

CHAPTER NINE

RELICS AND
REPRESENTATIONS

Not many whole ships have survived, but there are plenty of representations of them in a wide variety of forms; these can range from plans, to oil paintings, to scale models. There are many parts of ships which have also survived; these may be decorative features or items of their working equipment. They can be part of museums or private collections and there is a ready market in maritime antiques. Perhaps figureheads are regarded as the most significant because they are often seen to embody the character or the soul of the ship. Such is the demand that there are also businesses turning out replicas of these antiques.

From the nineteenth century, when a ship was first conceived it was designed on two-dimensional paper plans. When the general design was agreed, more detailed drawings were produced from which the shipbuilders could take measurements and begin to fabricate individual components. If the design was new, there may well have been another stage where a model of the proposed shape of the hull was built and tried out in an experimental test tank. The model was towed down the length of a long tank in which there was equipment to recreate different sea conditions. As the model was towed, its responses were carefully monitored and the data used to make any changes in the shape before building started. Tank testing is still used, but today much of the work has been taken over by computers with CAD (computer-aided design) software. This software can be used to create and plan the internal framing and layout in three dimensions. It can also produce programmes for the cutting machines to cut out the individual components from steel plates in the most economical way.

How such electronic records will be preserved in the future is anyone's guess, but there is a huge body of archive material representing older ships that have long gone to the breakers or the bottom of the ocean. Shipbuilders kept plans and details of the ships they built in case of repeat orders and as an archive of information that could help in future designs. The test-tank models on the other hand were fashioned from a hard wax which was usually melted down to make new models after the tests.

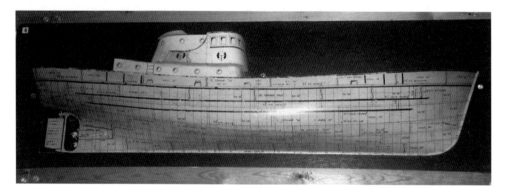

Top: Navies accumulated collections of models and trophies and many of these collections were eventually turned into maritime museums. They helped to teach new recruits the traditions of their service and instil a sense of pride through past achievements. The Musée des Petits Modèles at the Cherbourg Dockyard was a wonderfully mixed collection at the end of the nineteenth century with ship carvings (in the foreground), a training model of a late nineteenth-century battleship, builders' models, a model of an early steam engine and gear-cutting lathe.

Above: The half model was an essential design tool for shipbuilders before drawing up plans became the norm in the nineteenth century. It continued to be used by steel shipbuilders as a means of laying out the hull plating. All this can be carried out by computer today. In 1955 this half model was for a new design of fishing vessel that could be converted from a drifter into a trawler by Richards Ironworks at Lowestoft.

Opposite: Vessels from the past that have been scrapped or wrecked can be resurrected in miniature in the form of scale models. Malcolm Darch of Salcombe, the best of the professional model-makers at the moment, has been photographed completing a model of the fruit schooner *Zouave* of 1856. Before any part of its hull and fittings were built, Malcolm had to carry out extensive research and draw up a full set of plans.

Today, there are very few shipbuilding yards left in the British Isles, but for much of the nineteenth and twentieth centuries they supplied the rest of the world with merchant ships and warships. As individual yards closed, some of their plans were saved. John Brown & Co. (Clydebank) Ltd was the most famous shipyard on the River Clyde, which had the biggest concentration of shipbuilding yards anywhere in the world. John Brown built many famous ships, including the *Queen Mary*, the *Queen Elizabeth* and the *Queen Elizabeth II*. Plans of these and other ships have been preserved at Glasgow University, the Scottish Record Office, the National Maritime Museum and the Merseyside Maritime Museum. Plans of warships go back a lot further than plans for merchant ships. The Admiralty Collection of draughts goes back to the late seventeenth century and represents either new ships built in the Royal dockyards or ships that had been captured or bought for the Royal Navy. The oldest mercantile plans date from about 1772 and are from J.M. Hilhouse's shipyard at Bristol.

Model of H.M.S. "Hood."
Scale ³/₁₆" to the foot.

BASSETT-LOWKE LTD
MODEL MAKERS.
NORTHAMPTON.

This model, made by Basset Lowke in Northampton, was most likely made as a builder's model for John Brown & Co. at Clydebank or for the Admiralty. At a scale of ³/₁₆ in to the foot, the model would have been over 15 feet in length and showed HMS *Hood* in perfect detail in miniature.

Models built to a definite scale were often a substitute for designing on paper. A popular scale was a quarter of an inch to represent every foot. The Board of Admiralty commissioned very detailed un-rigged models of new designs from the mid-seventeenth century. But the half model was a far more widely used aid to ship design. The hull of a ship is symmetrical along its centre line and one half of the hull can represent the whole hull for design purposes. The shipbuilder would carve half a hull to scale to the agreed dimensions of his customer and to the most likely shape. This would aid discussions with the customer before building started. The shape of the frames of the ship could then be scaled off it and drawn out to full size, usually on a large flat floor known as the scrieve board and on which the wooden frames could be sawn. There were also half models for building iron or steel ships that were used to work out the dimensions and positions of the iron and steel plates of the hull. Many shipbuilders kept their half models for future reference and to decorate their offices. The practice also grew of making a decorative scale model of the ship that was presented to its ship-owner. These could be half models and in some case the half model was given a mirror at the back of its case which gave the illusion of it being 3D. Others were full models in glass cases on pedestals which could serve as publicity and prestige for the shipping company. This was particularly important to passenger liner operators and they might commission several models which could be toured at exhibitions or displayed in passenger agents' offices. At a scale of a quarter of an inch to a foot, a model of a large liner such as the *Mauretania* (32,000 tons) could measure up to 20 feet long and could be a considerable expense. Many of these models have found their way to maritime museums. There are models of the *Mauretania* to that scale in the Newcastle Discovery Museum, the National Maritime Museum and on the cruise liner *Queen Elizabeth II*. However none of these models, though to a precise scale, represent the ship as it would have been in reality. They are idealised versions; everything is pristine. All the fixtures and fittings, such as bollards and winches, have been gold or silver plated and the paint and varnish work has a mirror finish.

Model-making has also flourished outside shipyards. There have been professional model-makers and keen amateurs who have acquired a high standard of skill. Quite a lot of their work has involved recreating in miniature ships that have long ceased to sail. Many of the varied types of sailing ships are represented in museum collections by scale models. Malcolm Darch at Salcombe, who is probably one of the finest model-makers working today, will build you an exact miniature ship of almost any period and he will carry out the research and draw up plans to ensure that it is as accurate as possible. There are other model-makers who like to build their ships into realistic settings, under sail or alongside a dock wall. There are also many amateur model-makers who delight in building working radio-controlled models; some include real working steam engines and some are so large that the operator can sit inside the hull to sail them. There are also many survivors from the days when sailors made models at sea. Some of these were cunningly placed in bottles; others were more works of imagination than realistic – often with exaggerated masts and fictional names. They count as folk art rather than miniature ships.

Ships have also been represented on paper and canvas without the exactness of a scaled ship's plan. Royal ships were among the first to be depicted and Charles II's patronage of Dutch marine painters such as the Van de Veldes began a tradition of marine painting in Britain. At the start, the main subjects tended to be warships or the ships of the East India Co., which out-classed all other merchant ships in size and prestige. Some paintings celebrated their launch, others showed them under sail at sea or in action in a naval engagement. Depictions of other merchant ships became more common towards the end of the eighteenth century. The earliest painting of a named ship in the Merseyside Maritime Museum is that of the privateering brig *Viper*, returning to port with a captured French ship in 1781. This however was a special incident and no doubt the sale of such a large prize would have made the owners of the *Viper* a lot of money. More routine, peace-time portraits of merchant ships were commissioned by proud owners and masters. There were painters in the major ports who specialised in ship portraits. These 'pier head' artists often had to turn out paintings quickly while the ship was in port.

Above: Many ship-owners and ship masters took great pride in their ships and commissioned artists who specialised in ship pictures to paint their own ships. The commissioning owners or masters expected a painting that was very accurate. Quite often the ship would be depicted in two or more positions. This oil painting by Samuel Walters (the best of the Liverpool ship painters) shows the ship *Helen* entering the Mersey in the early 1840s.

Left: Paintings were not the only medium in which ships of the past have been represented. Ceramics decorated with pictures of specific ships were not uncommon. The late eighteenth-century Liverpool potteries produced blue and white Delftware punchbowls with a ship portrait inside. Similar bowls were produced to commission by the Danish makers of 'Elsinore' bowls in the nineteenth century. This pitcher was made and painted at the Herculaneum Pottery, Liverpool in 1813 and depicts the firm's own Mersey flat, the *Phebe*.

As a result they often worked to a formula, perhaps showing the ship under sail in three different positions in the same work. There were others, particularly Chinese artists undertaking the same kind of work in Far Eastern ports, who would produce a pair of pictures, one of the ship sailing in fair weather and the second in a tempest. The emphasis was always on producing a picture of the ship that was technically accurate. Steamer companies were also frequent patrons and built up large collections over many years. The Harrison Line, which closed its shipowning operations in 2002, had over a hundred pictures ranging from their earliest sailing brig to modern container ships and bulk carriers. They put them to good use because they were reproduced as calendars, posters and postcards as part of their marketing programme. Ship pictures are incredibly popular today and the old works, however primitive and formulaic, are collected avidly and new works are being produced in huge quantities, although of greatly varying quality.

Media other than canvas, paper or wood panels have also been used to depict ships; there are some notable punchbowls which have fine and accurate paintings of individual ships, such as the blue and white *Delftware* made in Liverpool in the mid-eighteenth century.

Relics are old things that have survived from the past and often a part of something that has been destroyed. They have been associated especially with the remains or possessions of saints or holy men and these relics became cult objects in their own right in the Middle Ages. Many were counterfeit and at the Reformation it was said that there were enough pieces of the True Cross to build a ship! Some ship relics carry some of the same connotations. The cult of the *Titanic* was strong even before the discovery of its wreck and has been reinforced by James Campbell's epic film. Books continue to be published about this infamous tragic accident in April 1912, and in 2004 there are two touring exhibitions, a temporary exhibition and three permanent displays about the ship. By association, any relic from its owners, the White Star Line, has increased hugely in value. A cup and saucer from an unknown White Star liner (admittedly made of the finest porcelain and elaborately decorated) was offered for sale at £700 in a recent ship enthusiast's fair.

Relics of old ships survive in a wide variety of shapes and sizes. Passenger liners are a major source and of great interest to many collectors. They can be ephemeral items such as menu cards or picture postcards, or portable items such as monogrammed crockery and tableware. These were sometimes taken by passengers as souvenirs, but more often they were sold off when the ship was broken up. Merseyside Maritime Museum was given a set of nickel-plated serving dishes and dish covers engraved with the White Star Line flag by a boys' boarding school. The school had bought them in a ship-breaker's auction in the 1920s. The ship chandlers who supplied T.&J. Harrison's ships with china found a complete pallet of their ships' ware when clearing out an old store. A full set was taken in for the same museum's collection and the rest was sold on to eager collectors and old Harrison employees. At the other end of the scale whole interiors have survived. The quality of the woodwork of many ships' public spaces has meant that they have been bought for use on land.

Ships' bells are among the most commonly preserved ship relics. This large example came from the wreck of the White Star liner *Oceanic* of 1899. It was the second ship of that name in the Line (the first was built in 1871) and the first ship to exceed the tonnage of the famous *Great Eastern*. The *Oceanic* was on patrol as an armed merchant cruiser in the 10th Squadron when it was wrecked on Foula Island in the Shetlands on 8 September 1914.

Right: Anchors are common relics and many have been trawled up by fishing vessels. Losing anchors through their cables breaking was once a common occurrence and it is usually impossible to ascribe them to a specific ship. This very large Admiralty-pattern anchor was one of those used to moor the training ship HMS *Conway* in the Menai Straits. It was recovered in 1986 to act as a 'signpost' to mark the entrance of the Maritime Museum at Liverpool.

Below: Relics of ships have frequently been recovered from their wrecks lying on the seabed. This can be contentious because some wrecks are also graves or have an archaeological importance. This propeller was from the Cunard liner *Lusitania*, which was sunk by a German submarine in contentious circumstances off Ireland in 1915.

The *Olympic*, the sister ship of the *Titanic*, was broken up at Jarrow on the Tyne in 1935. Much of its superbly carved and gilded panelling was salvaged and still survives. The staff of a paint factory at Hexham enjoy their tea breaks and meals surrounded by the *Olympic's* panelling, with a large stained-glass dome overhead.

There is even more of the *Olympic* at the Swan Hotel at Alnwick, where almost all the ground floor public rooms originated from her. Elsewhere much of the *Mauretania's* rich mahogany panels grace the Mauretania Bar in the centre of Bristol. Relics from the *Great Eastern*, which was broken up in 1889 at New Ferry on the Wirral, still turn up. Decorative dinner plates are still fairly common and there have also been garden benches fashioned from its teak deck planks, while a wonderful pub called the Great Eastern, overlooking the site of its destruction, has all sorts of panels and pedestal tables from the ship. Deck houses for the crew quarters, the galley and wheelhouses, from where the ship was steered, were usually made of good-quality hardwood and could be lifted clear of the ship. They made very acceptable summer houses or even living accommodation.

The working equipment and the fittings of a ship have also survived in large quantities. Most ships have brass fittings, such as port holes or binnacles (for holding a compass), and these have become highly sought after. The same is true for ship's wheels and bells. The traditional ship's wheel was an elaborate piece of joinery with turned spokes and inlays of brass. They have been displayed just as they are or converted into new uses, such as garden gates or hung from the ceiling with lamps as a sort of nautical chandelier. The demand for such relics has outstripped the supply and any originals are easily sold in the specialist maritime auctions. Firms such as Nauticalia have stepped in to fulfil the demand by making replica brass ship fittings and ship's wheels. Any vintage ship that possesses a wooden wheel usually takes steps to protect it from theft, such as taking the wheel away to storage while tied up in port! Brass items tend to survive well on shipwrecks and for many amateur wreck divers a brass port hole or something similar becomes a treasured souvenir.

Perhaps the most evocative of all such relics is the ship's bell with its name engraved on it. A ship's bell was used to mark the passage of time, with the twenty-four hours divided into six watches of four hours each. It could also be used as a fog signal where there was no other audible warning – such as a ship's siren or fog horn – carried on board. Although no longer of practical use, many ships carry them as a matter of tradition and to an extent, as with the figurehead, they have been seen to embody the 'soul' of the ship. Recently a naval diving team recovered the bell of the battleship *Prince of Wales* at no small expense. It had been sunk by Japanese aircraft off Singapore in the Second World War. Salvage divers had been spotted trying to free the bell and as a result action was taken to recover this important relic. It has been conserved and is now in the custody of the Royal Naval Museum. The Royal Navy normally prefers sunken warships to lie undisturbed because they are often the graves of drowned sailors.

Less decorative relics which document technical developments are important to museum collections. Full-size ship's engines, both steam and diesel (though usually of the smaller types), are to be found in many collections. Some specimens have their

Top: The ballroom of the White Star liner *Olympic* at the Swan Hotel at Alnwick is an even more spectacular example of reused panelling. As the *Olympic* was the sister ship of the ill-fated *Titanic*, it has a special importance.

Above left: Relics of ships can give a sense of scale and can explain the operation of ship's equipment, such as this tug's towing hook and tow rope.

Above right: Ship's clocks and instruments such as compasses are highly collectable and are the kind of equipment that is salvaged by shipbreakers and auctioned off. Some have important stories, such as the clock from the T class submarine HMS *Thetis* which sank on its trials with the loss of all but three of the crew.

Ships' panelling was usually made from high-quality woods such as mahogany with a high standard of finish. Much of it was sold off for reuse. The *Great Eastern* was broken up at New Ferry on the south bank of the Mersey in 1889 and the internal fittings were sold off. Quite a number of large pieces of the panelling can still be found in the adjacent Great Eastern pub.

Left: Another *Great Eastern* relic in the Great Eastern pub is this cast-iron pedestal table.

Opposite: This ship's model was made from a door of the liner it represents. It is rare to come across this type of memorabilia, but not impossible. Much was made of selling sections of planking (both teak and pine) from battleships and liners that had been converted into barrels, letter openers and other treen souvenirs.

WHITE STAR LINE R.M.S. "CEDRIC" 1903
MODEL TO SCALE OF 1 INCH = 100FEET MADE BY LESLIE WILSON
WITH WOOD FROM A FITTING OUT OF THE "CEDRIC" VIZ. A
MIDSHIPS PORT PASSAGEWAY DOOR FOUND AT FELIN DRE
NEWMARKET, FLINTSHIRE 1939, 'CEDRIC' HAVING BEEN
BROKEN UP IN 1932

cylinders and valve chests cut away to show their internal workings and are turned by compressed air or electric motors. Such engines have often been teaching aids in marine engineering colleges rather than taken from a ship. Ships' equipment can be important for museum displays because it can give visitors a sense of the huge size of ships compared with other man-made objects. Navigational and communications equipment found on the bridge of ships since the 1940s include radar consoles, Decca navigators and VHF radio sets; all have been seen as important acquisitions for they show the revolution that electronics brought about at sea both for navigation and for warfare.

Sometimes, old ships' components can be reused. These can be from other ships of the same type, so, for example, many of the Thames barges that have been re-rigged in recent years have winches and spars taken from older barges that have been hulked. The mizzen mast from the training ship HMS *Conway* has been re-erected as a memorial to the ship but also as part of the landscaping of a derelict dock area. Other maritime relics such as anchors and ships' propellers have also been displayed as pieces of public sculpture. Engines have been bought from the old ships and reused in new ships or even ashore. For many years Salters, the makers of weighing scales in Birmingham, had a MAN U-boat diesel engine to power their emergency electricity generator.

Perhaps figureheads are among the most nostalgic of all ship's relics. They are invariably carved in wood and many have rotted away after their initial preservation. Those that remain are highly prized and the best examples are held by maritime museums. Some have been salvaged from shipwrecks, such as the large collection displayed at the Shipwreck Museum on Tresco in the Isles of Scilly. The vicious rocks around this group of islands trapped many fine sailing ships and the Dorrien-Smith family, owners of Tresco, built up a fine collection of nineteenth-century ship carvings. This is maintained by the National Maritime Museum – such is its importance.

Sometimes ships' relics are cast off and are found new uses almost by accident. This companionway has been adapted as a shelter and even labelled 'Casa Mia' (my house) at the Grytviken whaling station on South Georgia Island.

Some ships' equipment has been rescued for reuse in restoring old ships. This Elliott & Garrood steam capstan for hauling herring driftnets is awaiting installation at the Excelsior shipyard, Lowestoft.

Ship decoration reached its most elaborate in the seventeenth- and early eighteenth-century warships. It was an expression of power and prestige and was often carried from the bow along the sides to the stern. This model of HMS *St George*, a 100-gun ship of 1714, has a life-size carving of a leaping horse and knight supporting the royal coat of arms with equally elaborate supporting scroll work below and classically correct pilasters behind it.

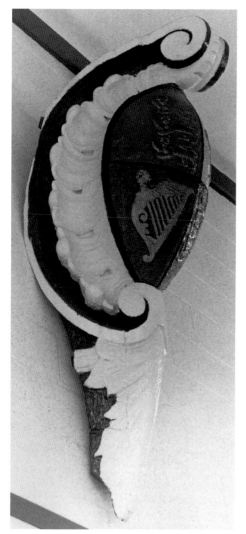

Left: The cost of such carvings became prohibitive and by 1750 the Admiralty ordained much simplified designs. This simple badge of the royal coat of arms was carried by Victorian frigate HMS *Calliope* and is displayed at the Royal Naval Reserve depot at Gateshead.

Right: Lions, with their qualities of power and fierceness, were a very suitable subject for warships' figureheads. This late seventeenth- or possibly early eighteenth-century example is rather stylised and lacking in fierceness. It ended up as the sign for the Red Lion inn at Mendlesham, Suffolk.

Owners of sailing ships often took a deep pride in their ownership and would commission figureheads of themselves or members of their family, friends or business associates. According to the size of the ship and the amount of money expended, they could be a bust, as in the case of this unknown mid-Victorian gent, three-quarter length or full length down to their feet.

Above: The early steamers followed the tradition of mounting a figurehead. The 703-ton wooden paddle steamer *Sirius* was built as a coastal packet for services between London and Cork. In 1838 it was hired to cross the Atlantic, which it accomplished in seventeen days – the first transatlantic crossing under steam power alone. Its figurehead of a dog is preserved at the Hull Maritime Museum and derives from *Sirius*, nicknamed the 'dog star'.

Opposite: Straight instead of clipper bows became the norm for iron-hulled steamers. There were exceptions, such as the beautiful steam yacht *Nahlin* of 1930. It became the Romanian royal and later presidential yacht and latterly a floating restaurant. It has been brought back to Liverpool for restoration by its new owner.

Previous page:

Left: A female warrior in Scottish garb representing the Spirit of Scotland. It adorned the bow of the *Caledonia* of Arbroath which was wrecked at Morwenstow, Cornwall in 1842. The figurehead was erected in the local churchyard to mark the grave of the *Caledonia*'s drowned crewmen.

Right: The figurehead of *The First of May* was of the three-quarter (or demi) type. Her costume dates her to the 1840s and, although quite crudely carved, her face has been carved from life. Perhaps the ship-owner's daughter posed for this three-dimensional portrait.

Other figureheads have been salvaged from ship-breakers' yards. The late Sydney Cumbers amassed an important collection from ship-breakers working around the Thames and displayed them in his house at Gravesend overlooking that river. His widow passed his collection on to the *Cutty Sark*, where they are displayed in the hold.

The origins of figureheads appear to go back to the roots of seafaring when bow ornaments symbolised a propitiation of the sea gods or were a charm against ill fortune. British examples may perhaps hark back to such distant superstitions, but they seem to owe more to a need for display of prestige or a pride in ownership. Realistic wood carvings of the type found on ships seem to date back to the Renaissance. Some of the finest work was to be found on the large sailing battleships of the seventeenth and early eighteenth centuries, which were decorated with a riot of carvings from bow to stern at prodigious expense. The figurehead was always the focus and many warships of this period featured a leaping lion. The lion, as King of the Beasts, was a symbol of power, domination and fierceness, which are all appropriate qualities for a warship. One lion figurehead survives in the most unusual location: on the wall of the Red Lion pub at Martlesham in Suffolk. No one is quite sure how it came to be there, but there is no doubt that it originally came from an early eighteenth-century warship. The cost of ship carvings caused the Admiralty to restrict later sailing warships to figureheads alone and a significant number have survived in naval dockyards and depots. For example, the figurehead of HMS *Eaglet*, a seventy-four-gun warship which became a floating base at Liverpool, was saved when the ship was scrapped in 1927 and is still displayed at the Royal Naval Reserve at Brunswick Dock, Liverpool.

Merchant ships usually carried figureheads that reflected the name of the ship. Shipowning was often a family business and a new ship might be named after a member of the family or possibly the owner himself. Others might be named after popular fictional characters. The *Cutty Sark* (short shirt) owes its name to Robert Burns' poem *Tam o' Shanter* and its figurehead is that of Nannie the Witch reaching out to grasp the tail of Tam's horse. Others represent Greek or Roman gods or symbolise abstract qualities such as Hope or Progress. Animals and birds were less popular than human figures. A ship-owner who needed to watch his costs could reduce the price by choosing a bust or a three-quarter-length figurehead as opposed to a full-length piece. Some opted for an abstract scroll and there were ship carvers who could turn out a standardised figure for as little as £3. Ship carvers tended to be found close to shipbuilding centres and supplied not only figureheads but also decorative carvings for the sterns and interiors of ships. It must be admitted that some of the surviving examples are quite crude in their anatomy and in their carving; this was especially true on the smaller coastal ships.

As iron steamers came to prominence, the old form of curved 'clipper' bow gave way to a straight one. This had no place for a carved figurehead and as sailing ships stopped being built at the end of the nineteenth century, this traditional decoration all but died out. However, it did survive on luxury vessels such as steam yachts where the emphasis was on producing a beautiful ship and in recent years the craft of carving figureheads has undergone a revival. This is partly due to the demand for restoring historic ships to their original appearance and partly due to a general revival of interest in handicrafts in these days of mass production. Surviving figureheads are a striking visual reminder of the romance of seafaring, when ships were among the most beautiful of Man's creations. At the same time, they carry an air of sadness because their ships which carried them proudly on their bows have all gone.

BIBLIOGRAPHY

INDEX

BIBLIOGRAPHY

Baddeley, Jon, *Nautical Antiques and Collectables*, Sothebys Publications, London, 1993

Ballard, Robert and Archbold, Rick, *Lost Liners*, Hodder and Stoughton, London, 1997

Bound, Mensun, *The Archaeology of Ships of War* (2 volumes) Anthony Nelson, Oswestry, 1995 and 1998

Brouwer, Norman, *The International Register of Historic Ships*, Chatham Publishing, London, 1999

Buxton, Ian and Dalziel, Nigel, *Shipbreaking at Morecambe: T.W. Ward Ltd 1905 – 1933*, Lancaster City Museums, 1993

Buxton, Ian, *Metal Industries* (shipbreaking at Rosyth and Charlestown), World Ship Society, Kendal, 1997

Corlett, Ewan, *The Iron Ship: The History and Significance of Brunel's* Great Britain, Moonraker Press, Bradford-on-Avon, 1988

Darch, Malcolm, *Modelling Maritime History*, David and Charles, Newton Abbot, 1988

Delgado, James (ed.), *British Museum Encyclopaedia of Underwater and Maritime Archaeology*, British Museum Press, London, 1997

Emmerson, George, *The Greatest Iron Ship: SS* Great Eastern, David and Charles, Newton Abbot, *c.*1980

Gardiner, Robert and Greenhill, Basil (eds), *Conway's History of the Ship* (12 volumes), Conway Maritime Press, London, 1993

Greenhill, Basil, *The Archaeology of Boats and Ships: An Introduction*, Conway Maritime Press, 1995

Kemp, Peter (ed.), *The Oxford Companion to Ships and the Sea*, Oxford University Press, 1992

Mannering, Julian, *The Chatham Directory of Inshore Craft*, Chatham Publishing, London, 1997

Marsden, Peter, *Ships and Shipwrecks*, Batsford/English Heritage, London, 1997

Stammers, Michael, *Figureheads*, Shire Publications, Princes Risborough, 1990

Welles-Henderson, J. and Carlisle, Rodney P., *Marine Art and the Sailor's Life 1750 – 1910*, Antique Collector's Club, Woodbridge, 1999

INDEX

If you are interested in purchasing
other books published by Tempus, or in case you have
difficulty finding any Tempus books in your local bookshop,
you can also place orders directly through our website

www.tempus-publishing.com